A Catholic Scientist
Champions the Shroud of Turin

Also by Dr. Gerard M. Verschuuren
from Sophia Institute Press:

Forty Anti-Catholic Lies
A Mythbusting Apologist
Sets the Record Straight

In the Beginning
A Catholic Scientist Explains
How God Made Earth Our Home

A Catholic Scientist Proves God Exists

How Science Points to God

Dr. Gerard M. Verschuuren

A Catholic Scientist Champions the Shroud of Turin

SOPHIA INSTITUTE PRESS
Manchester, New Hampshire

Sophia Institute Press
Box 5284, Manchester, NH 03108
1-800-888-9344

www.SophiaInstitute.com

Sophia Institute Press® is a registered trademark of Sophia Institute.

Library of Congress Cataloging-in-Publication Data

Names: Verschuuren, G. M. N. (Geert M. N.), author.
Title: A Catholic scientist champions the Shroud of Turin / by Dr. Gerard M. Verschuuren.
Description: Manchester, NH : Sophia Institute Press, [2020] Includes bibliographical references and index. Summary: "Examines biblical, historical, and scientific evidence for the authenticity of the Shroud of Turin"— Provided by publisher.
Identifiers: LCCN 2020037482 (print) LCCN 2020037483 (ebook) ISBN 9781644133200 (paperback) ISBN 9781644133217 (ebook)
Subjects: LCSH: Holy Shroud. Religion and science.
Classification: LCC BT587.S4 V47 2020 (print) LCC BT587.S4 (ebook) DDC 232.96/6—dc23
LC record available at https://lccn.loc.gov/2020037482
LC ebook record available at https://lccn.loc.gov/2020037483

First printing

To
all scientists who have
defended the authenticity of
the Shroud of Turin

Contents

Preface

The Shroud of Turin has become a very controversial topic during the past few decades, with opinions about it varying widely. For those on one end of the spectrum, it is merely a piece of cloth that was perhaps painted by a very talented artist — an *icon* of a crucified person, at best. For those at the other end, it is a *relic* that they venerate dearly as the authentic burial cloth of Jesus Christ, the Savior of humanity.

Who is right? Who has the authority to decide? Nowadays, most people would declare science the best referee, but does science really deserve the final say?

Even aside from its theological significance, the Shroud of Turin is a puzzling object of scientific investigation. The purely scientific approach may seem incompatible with the deeply religious nature of the Shroud, but the apparent clash doesn't discard the value of experimental testing. Science may very well be able to help us determine the authenticity of the Shroud of Turin. It may help us discover whether the Shroud is indeed, as believers claim, the Shroud of Jesus, worthy of veneration. If it is not, then the faithful no longer have a relic but only an icon.

In this book, we will carefully balance the scientific approach and the religious approach. We will weigh the claims that science makes for and against the authenticity of the Shroud of Turin. We will assess what those claims are worth in the light of what we know through faith, so that we may develop a more reliable and accurate perception of the Shroud. The Catholic Church is known for balancing the input of both faith and reason, and thus, in this manner, we will set out to study the puzzling object.

Let me reveal in advance that through my own investigations of the science behind the Shroud of Turin, I have come to appreciate more and more the credentials of this amazing burial cloth. Let me guide you on my journey of discovery from the Shroud of Turin to the Shroud of Jesus of Nazareth, the Messiah.

A Catholic Scientist
Champions the Shroud of Turin

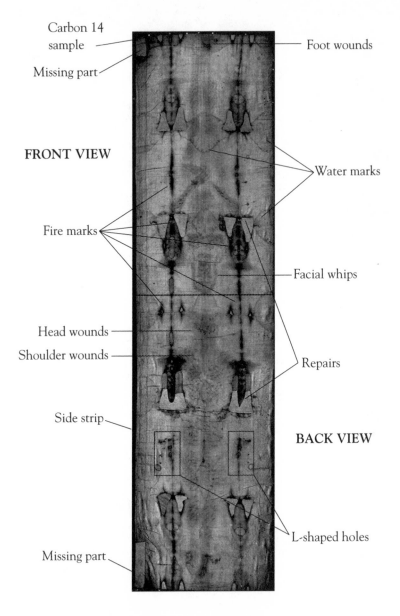

Carbon 14 sample

Missing part

FRONT VIEW

Fire marks

Head wounds

Shoulder wounds

Side strip

Missing part

Foot wounds

Water marks

Facial whips

Repairs

BACK VIEW

L-shaped holes

FULL-LENGTH IMAGE OF THE SHROUD OF TURIN

1

In Search of Arbitration

Is the Shroud of Turin the burial cloth of Jesus, or is it not? This key question will guide our study. Who, or what, will be the arbiter in this debate? For some it is science; for others it is faith. Who is right? Are they both?

Faith and Reason

The Catholic Church has a longstanding tradition of endorsing what is called the twosome of faith and reason. As Pope St. John Paul II famously said, "Faith and reason are like two wings on which the human spirit rises to the contemplation of truth."[1] In other words, we find the truth by using both faith and reason. *Truth* is the key word here. "One may define the human being, therefore, as the one who seeks the truth."[2]

There is a delicate balance between faith and reason. One cannot be without the other. In other words, there is no faith without some form of reason, and there is no reason without

---

[1] John Paul II, encyclical letter *Fides et Ratio* (September 14, 1998), introduction.
[2] Ibid., no. 28.

some form of faith. This may sound strange to some people, so let's find out why it must be.

On the one hand, there is no faith without some form of reason. Many people nowadays think that faith and reason have nothing to do with each other. They consider faith, especially religious faith, as something you just have to believe in without any reasonable foundation. They see religious faith as a leap into the irrational, devoid of any reasoning—a form of "blind faith." This, however, contradicts Church teaching. St. Augustine explained, "Believers are also thinkers: in believing, they think and in thinking, they believe."[3] He introduced his two famous formulas, which express the coherent synthesis between faith and reason: "Believe so you may understand" (*crede ut intelligas*), but also, and inseparably, "Understand so you may believe" (*intelligere ut credas*).[4]

Centuries later, Pope John Paul II would repeat this synthesis when he deemed it "necessary to stress the unity of truth and thus the positive contribution which rational knowledge can and must make to faith's knowledge."[5] With these words, he reiterated the Church's longstanding tradition affirming the relationship between faith and reason—a feature distinct from other religions. The Catholic Church does not see the two as competitors or contestants, but rather as participants in the same search for truth, even in matters of religious faith.

Obviously, there is much more to religious faith than the belief that God exists, yet reason still plays a role beyond that basic belief. St. Thomas Aquinas summarizes the relationship

---

[3] Augustine, *De Praedestinatione Sanctorum* 2, 5: PL 44, 963.
[4] Augustine, *Sermon* 43, 7, 9.
[5] John Paul II, *Fides et Ratio*, no. 53.

succinctly: (1) reason prepares the mind for faith; (2) reason explains the truths of faith; and (3) reason defends the truths of faith.[6] In short, reason supports faith, and faith without reason can mislead easily.

On the other hand, there is no reason without some form of faith. To reason properly, we need logic as a starting point. We need faith in the rules of logic, faith in the premises we often start from, faith in the validity of rational conclusions. G. K. Chesterton liked to ask his readers this disturbing question: "Why should not good logic be as misleading as bad logic?"[7] No one would answer that good logic is as misleading as bad logic. Hence, we need some form of faith in good logic. The power of logic is something you need to believe in before you can use it.

Furthermore, if a human being is indeed a reasoning being —traditionally referred to as *animal rationale*—we need belief in the human capacity of reasoning. We are constantly employing our reason throughout our lives. Each time we engage in a discussion or a dispute, we use reasoning to defend our position or to explain why we disagree with the position of others. Each time we come up with any kind of explanation, we use reasoning. Reasoning is part of our intellectual nature—a nature in which we must have faith. It gives us access to the "unseen" world of thoughts, laws, and truths—all of which require faith.

From this we may conclude that faith and reason keep each other in tow. Pope John Paul II unites them when he says, "Reason and faith cannot be separated without diminishing the capacity of men and women to know themselves, the world and God

---

[6] Especially in Thomas Aquinas, *Super Boethium de Trinitate*, q. 2, art. 3, response.

[7] G. K. Chesterton, *Orthodoxy* (Chicago: Moody, 2009), 33.

in an appropriate way."[8] To show their unison even further, he adds, "Faith asks that its object be understood with the help of reason; and at the summit of its searching reason acknowledges that it cannot do without what faith presents."[9]

The twosome of faith and reason, therefore, makes for an important and legitimate *distinction*, but unfortunately, as Pope John Paul II warns us, "the legitimate distinction between the two forms of learning [have become] more and more a fateful *separation*.... Another of the many consequences of this separation was an ever deeper mistrust with regard to reason itself. In a spirit both skeptical and agnostic, some began to voice a general mistrust, which led some to focus more on faith and others to deny its rationality altogether."[10] One of the reasons explaining the trend toward separation is the dramatic rise of rationalism and the dependency on the field of scientific research.

Religion and Science

Thinking in terms of faith and reason may not sound very appealing to people with a modern mindset; rather, they would like to speak in terms of religion and science, given the spectacular achievements of science. Well, there may not be a problem with that adaptation, but we need to be aware of some caveats.

First of all, those who make this move tend to create some dangerous implications. They often link reason exclusively with science, as if the only legitimate role of reason is to be found in science. Conversely, they suggest that religion is only a matter of

[8]   John Paul II, *Fides et Ratio*, no. 16.
[9]   Ibid., no. 42.
[10]   Ibid., no. 45 (italics added).

6

"pure" or "blind" faith, excluding the role of reason in religion. This understanding implies that there is no faith to be found in science and no reason in religion—a very confusing and misleading implication.

To reiterate, reason should play a role in faith, and therefore also in religion. On the other hand, even in science there is faith involved as well, arguably even religious faith. Science without faith is impossible; we need faith in our senses, faith in our intellect, faith in logic and math, faith in our memories, and faith in what others have discovered. Besides, we need some form of faith in the scientific enterprise itself because it is based on a series of assumptions—all of which require some form of faith: faith in the power of reason, faith that we can comprehend our world, faith that the world is not capricious and unpredictable, faith that we live in a world of "law and order," faith that like causes have like effects—the list goes on and on.

Assumptions like these are "hidden," as most of an iceberg is hidden under water, yet they play a fundamental role in science. They must be there before science can even get started, for without them science could not get off the ground. In other words, science is something you need to believe in before you can practice it: it requires faith. If science attempted to justify its own presuppositions, it would be engaging in circular reasoning.

Second, when people of faith think that their religious beliefs are sacrosanct, untouchable, and unshakable, they are claiming something that is indefensible. Why should we believe in religious claims? Not because it feels good, not because it sounds attractive, not because it is the majority view. The only valid reason is this: because it is *true*. Therefore, we need reasonable arguments to defend religious beliefs as well. Certainly, there is more to faith than that which can be backed up by logical reasoning and evidence, but in order to avoid falling into fideism, one must acknowledge the worth and necessity of reason when pursuing truth.

The same holds for science; we accept what science tells us because we think it is true. This makes some believe that science contains the only legitimate tools to discover truth—hence their belief that their scientific findings are sacrosanct, untouchable, and unshakable. However, the history of science tells us differently. Science is a fallible enterprise; what seems to be true today may turn out to be false tomorrow.

Nevertheless, the misunderstood distinction between faith and reason was carried over to the fatal *separation* between scientific knowledge and other kinds of knowledge—namely, moral, metaphysical, and religious knowledge. As Pope John Paul II noted, "In the field of scientific research, a positivistic mentality took hold which not only abandoned the Christian vision of the world, but more especially rejected every appeal to a metaphysical or moral vision."[11] As a result, scientific beliefs claimed a victory over religious beliefs—at least in the minds of many nowadays.

Third, in contrast to this misleading development, we should make the case that there are various kinds of truths. Pope John Paul II distinguishes at least three modes of truth. As he puts it, "Most of them depend upon immediate evidence or are confirmed by experimentation. This is the mode of truth proper to everyday life and to scientific research. At another level we find philosophical truth, attained by means of the speculative powers of the human intellect. Finally, there are religious truths which are to some degree grounded in philosophy, and which we find in the answers which the different religious traditions offer to the

[11] John Paul II, *Fides et Ratio*, no. 46.

ultimate questions."[12] If this is correct, then scientific truths are only one kind of truth, in addition to philosophical and religious.

For the purpose of our discussion, we will not go into philosophical truths but will consider only two of these types of truth: truth as found in religion (e.g., the Incarnation and the Virgin Birth) and truth as found in science (e.g., gravity and metabolism). What unites both kinds of truths is the fact that truth is truth, whether we like it or not, whether we feel it or not, whether others enforce it or not. Truth is something beyond human control, for beliefs cannot change the truth. If the earth is not flat, believing that it is does not make it flat. Similarly, believing that God does not exist cannot make God disappear. In either case, we are dealing with truths and facts. G.K. Chesterton asserted "that truth exists whether we like it or not, and that it is for us to accommodate ourselves to it," not the other way around.[13]

Once we admit that truth is truth, there is no longer room for so-called double truth. One cannot have one thing being true in one area and false in another, or true at one point in time and false at another point. Truth is truth—always and everywhere—for all truth is God's truth. So, there's no real opposition between the truths of reason and science versus the truths of faith and religion. If there seems to be an opposition, then it can only be a deceiving one.

St. Thomas Aquinas explicitly dealt with the issue of "double truth," which entails the idea that a notion could be true in faith and religion and, at the same time, false according to reason and science. Instead, Aquinas asserted that what we know through reason can never be in conflict with what we know through faith,

---

[12] Ibid., no. 30.
[13] G.K. Chesterton, *Illustrated London News*, June 8, 1907.

and what we know through faith can never be in violation of what we know through reasoning. In his own words, "[The] truth that the human reason is naturally endowed to know cannot be opposed to the truth of the Christian faith."[14] These two sources of information can never be in conflict with each other—so long as we understand them correctly—because God is the Author of both. They are acquired in different ways, however—for instance, through the history of God's revelation (in religion) or through experimental testing (in science).

Fourth, what we call truth, either in science or religion, may turn out to be *not* truth but an error. We find this both in science and in religion. An example from science is the theory of geocentrism, which states that the sun revolves around the earth. Although popularly held for thousands of years, geocentrism was, and is, false. In other words, it was never true, but we thought that it was for a while. Another example from science is the theory that the universe is eternal—that is, without a beginning and an end. Even Albert Einstein held this theory for a while, until he had to accept Fr. Georges Lemaître's theory that the universe had a beginning; this later became known as the Big Bang Theory. There are many more examples in science, but the general idea is clear: what is thought to be true today in science may turn out to be false tomorrow.

Something relatively similar could be said about religion. Although it is true that dogmas in the Catholic religion do not change, they may have undergone a process of gradual development and precision. Roy Schoeman gave a good description of this process:

---

[14] Thomas Aquinas, *Summa contra Gentiles* 1, 7, 6–7.

Abraham was given a fuller knowledge of God, and a greater intimacy with him, than any of his predecessors had since the Fall. Then, when God revealed himself to Moses in the burning bush, he gave Moses a yet fuller revelation of the divine Name, which had been with-held from mankind until then.... Similarly, the Messianic prophecies in the Old Testament contain veiled information about the Messiah that became clear only later, through the life of Jesus himself and through the inspiration of the Gospel writers. And so it is throughout the rest of salvation history.[15]

A similar development happened when God revealed Himself in Jesus, exposing the triune God, one God in three Persons. The dogma of the Trinity had not yet been revealed to the Jews until Jesus Christ came along. All Paul's letters and all four Gospels do clearly mention that Jesus was the Son of God, but it took longer, and the help of the Holy Spirit, to know the full truth of all of this: "These things I have spoken to you, while I am still with you. But the Counselor, the Holy Spirit, whom the Father will send in my name, he will teach you all things, and bring to your remembrance all that I have said to you."[16]

Fifth, we end up with a delicate balance between the two: science and reason can never claim what is against religion and faith, and religion and faith can never claim anything that is against science or reason; that would amount to a form of "double truth." In contrast, there are questions that science cannot answer, in the same way as there are questions that religion cannot

---

[15] Roy Schoeman, *Salvation Is from the Jews* (San Francisco: Ignatius Press, 2003), 80.

[16] John 14:25–26.

answer. Therefore, religious issues cannot be solved by science, and scientific issues cannot be solved by religion. Each has its own authority but also its own limitations.

Because of these limited fields, religion has the right and the duty to question what science claims when it comes to matters of faith and morals. Science, in turn, has the right and the duty to question what religion claims in matters outside of faith and morals. It is an important dialogue to ensure that we move toward the truth at all times.

From this discussion follows an important insight. Whatever we think we know through religion may give us reason to question that which we think we know through science. And reversed, whatever we think we know through science may give us reason to question that which we think we know through religion.

The Religion and Science of the Shroud of Turin

Back to the original question that we posed at the beginning of this chapter: who or what is the arbiter in controversies about the Shroud of Turin? Is it faith *or* reason? No, it is faith *and* reason. Is it religion *or* science? No, it is religion *and* science. The Shroud of Turin is not the exclusive territory of science, nor is it the exclusive territory of faith. They both have their own specific part to play in the investigation. Neither one has answers to all our questions.

The previous sections have made it very clear: we cannot believe just anything about the Shroud, not even if it is a deeply felt religious belief about its authenticity as the burial cloth of Jesus Christ. Religious beliefs cannot go against reason, nor can they be in contradiction with what we know from other sources, such as science. Those who believe the Shroud of Turin is the burial cloth of Jesus believe so because it is true, and nothing less. Therefore, in the rest of this book, we need to test our beliefs, both scientific and religious, about the Shroud of Turin.

To do so, we intend to use reasonable arguments to defend, or perhaps question, both religious *and* scientific claims about the Shroud of Turin. Each claim ought to honor the twosome of faith and reason as well as the twosome of religion and science.

It remains important to remember that science can tell us something about the Shroud that religious faith cannot, and religious faith can tell us something about the Shroud that science cannot. Nevertheless, in whatever they tell us, faith and science can never contradict one another. If they do, either one or both of them must be in error. This longstanding teaching of the Catholic Church is probably best described and defended by one of the most renowned Doctors of the Church, St. Thomas Aquinas, in the words we heard earlier: "[The] truth that the human reason is naturally endowed to know cannot be opposed to the truth of the Christian faith."[17]

If we believe that the Shroud of Turin is the burial cloth of Jesus, but science tells us that it is a forgery, then either our faith is wrong, our science is wrong, or both are wrong. But they cannot both be true—that would go against reason. So, when science claims—based on historical analysis, computer analysis, anatomical analysis, textile analysis, pollen analysis, carbon analysis, blood analysis, or DNA analysis—that the Shroud cannot be more than a millennium old, religious faith has the right and the duty to question the claims' validity.

On the other hand, what faith claims about the Shroud may not be confirmed by scientific tests, but it still can be true and

---

[17] Thomas Aquinas, *Summa contra Gentiles* 1, 7, 6–7.

valid. Faith has the right to claim that the Shroud of Turin is the authentic burial cloth of Jesus, even when science cannot confirm it, as long as science does not contradict it on undisputable grounds.

Apparently, arbitration about the Shroud of Turin is more complicated than many people think. It's certainly not a black-and-white case. There are no one-sided answers—for those are what they are: "one-sided," that is, only a part of the full answer. Science may know more about the Shroud of Turin than religious faith knows or may ever know. In turn, religious faith may know more about the Shroud of Turin than science knows or may ever know. Let's find out which may be the case.

2

Biblical Analysis

The Shroud of Turin is claimed to be the linen burial cloth in which Jesus of Nazareth was wrapped after His Crucifixion — an event that has been corroborated by numerous historical accounts, both biblical and nonbiblical. The Crucifixion's historical credibility confounds some, as the event is, in the words of St. Paul, "a stumbling block to Jews and folly to Gentiles."[18] Yet, here are some early accounts from the non-Christian world:

- In his writings on Emperor Nero, Tacitus (ca. 56–ca. 120), a Roman senator and historian of the Roman Empire, explicitly mentions Jesus and His followers, saying, "Christus, from whom the name had its origin, suffered the extreme penalty during the reign of Tiberius at the hands of ... Pontius Pilatus, procurator of Judea."[19]

- Josephus (ca. 37–ca. 100), a Romano-Jewish historian who was born in Jerusalem, wrote about Jesus: "At this time, there was a wise man who was called Jesus.... And many people from among the Jews and other nations

---

[18] 1 Cor. 1:23.
[19] Tacitus, *Annals* 15, 44.

became his disciples. Pilate condemned him to be crucified and to die."[20]

- Pliny the Younger (ca. 62–ca. 113), the Roman gov-
ernor of Bithynia in Asia Minor, wrote in one of his
letters to Emperor Trajan, dated around 112, what he
had learned about the Christians: "They were in the
habit of meeting on a certain fixed day before it was
light, when they sang in alternate verses a hymn to
Christ, as to a god."[21]

- Lucian of Samosata (ca. 125–ca. 180), a Greek satirist,
wrote sneeringly about the early Christians as follows:
"The Christians ... worship a man to this day—the
distinguished personage who introduced their novel rites
—and was crucified on that account."[22]

- Suetonius (ca. 69–ca. 122), a Roman historian, never
referred to Jesus' Crucifixion, but he did mention that a
man named Chrestus [sic] had started a movement that
reached as far as Rome: "Since the Jews constantly made
disturbances at the instigation of Chrestus, he [Claudius]
expelled them from Rome."[23]

It is hard to deny these historical facts. Nevertheless, the main
information we have about Jesus' Crucifixion comes from the New
Testament. What does the Bible tell us about the Crucifixion?

[20] Josephus, *Antiquities* 18, 63–64.
[21] Pliny, *Letters*, trans. William Melmoth, rev. W. M. L. Hutchinson
(Cambridge, MA: Harvard University Press, 1935), 2:10.96.
[22] Lucian, "The Death of Peregrine," in *The Works of Lucian of
Samosata* (Oxford: Clarendon Press, 1949), 4:11–13 (italics
original).
[23] Suetonius, *Lives of the Caesars*, trans. Catharine Edwards (Oxford: Oxford University Press, 2009), 184.

What We Know about the Crucifixion of Jesus

It may come as a surprise that the Bible is exceptionally brief about the details of Jesus' Crucifixion. The Cross of Jesus is a central symbol in the narrative of Christianity, yet the description of the Crucifixion in the Gospels is rather short. All four Gospels do mention the Crucifixion, though basically in the same terms, with only minor differences. They report the Crucifixion as a historical fact that changed the world, but for some reason, they leave it at that.

There is much discussion as to when the Crucifixion took place. The Synoptic Gospels (Matthew, Mark, and Luke) report that Jesus was crucified on the fifteenth day of the month of Nisan—a day later than the date given in the Gospel of John. One of the reasons there is no real consensus is that there are different calendars in question—Hebrew, Qumran, Julian, and Gregorian. According to the British physicist Colin Humphreys, the Last Supper occurred on the Wednesday before Christ's Crucifixion in AD 33, rather than on the Thursday with which it is traditionally associated. Again, inconsistencies such as this one may be attributed to varying calendars in use by the Gospel writers at the time. From the evidence, it appears that Matthew, Mark, and Luke recorded the events according to the Samaritan calendar of older, Egyptian influence, whereas John's account aligns with the Jewish one—a newer Babylonian-influenced calendar (both of which are still used today).[24]

Humphreys proposed the date of the Crucifixion to be April 3, 33, in the Julian calendar, which would be April 1, 33, in the

---

[24] Colin J. Humphreys, *The Mystery of the Last Supper: Reconstructing the Final Days of Jesus* (Cambridge: Cambridge University Press, 2011), 193.

Gregorian calendar. However, the year 33 would be too late for the Crucifixion if we assume—as is reasonable and common among scholars—that Jesus was born in the year 4 BC. According to St. Matthew, Jesus was born during the days of Herod.[25] This means that Jesus could not have been born any later than the spring of 4 BC, when Herod died. We know that Jesus lived some thirty-three years because St. Luke tells us that "Jesus, when he began his ministry, was about thirty years of age."[26] In John's Gospel, after His Baptism, Jesus attended at least three annual Passover feasts.[27] So, at the shortest, His ministry would have lasted some three years. This means His Crucifixion would have occurred around AD 30. But let's leave this entire "iffy" discussion for what it's worth.

Back to our original question: What could be the reason for the brevity of the biblical account of the Crucifixion? We need to be aware that, in a way, crucifixion was for Jesus' time what the electric chair is for our age. Although the Crucifixion is definitely mentioned in the Bible, it is easy to understand that its writers did not want to go into detail about this kind of execution. Instead, the first Christians wanted to know primarily *what* led to Jesus' Crucifixion, *why* He voluntarily accepted this inhumane form of execution, and *how* His Crucifixion could be part of His announcement of the good news. The Bible is much more detailed, therefore, about the events leading up to Jesus' death and the reason why the Crucifixion is so fundamental to Christianity than it is about the Crucifixion itself. It is also worth remembering that the Gospel writers did not have the

---

[25] Matt. 2:1.
[26] Luke 3:23.
[27] John 2:13; 6:4; 11:55.

intention of writing a strictly historical account but rather a rich, sacred text.

The New Testament reveals that the Crucifixion made redemption and salvation possible for all of humanity. When the priests and Pharisees saw what Jesus was doing and heard what He was preaching, they called together the Sanhedrin,[28] a council with seventy-one members, including the leading Pharisees as well as the Sadducees, who worked in the Temple. It was led by the high priest at the time, Joseph Caiaphas. He prophesied to all the members of the council just before Jesus was sentenced to death: "You do not understand that it is expedient for you that one man should die for the people, and that the whole nation should not perish." St. John explicitly adds, "He did not say this of his own accord, but being high priest that year he prophesied that Jesus should die for the nation."[29]

Why does *one* person need to die for *all*? The biblical answer is that all of humanity had been corrupted by sin and could be redeemed only by someone both human *and* divine: the Son of God. As the Letter to the Hebrews puts it, "It is impossible that the blood of bulls and goats should take away sins."[30] The Son of God achieved what no one else and no amount of sacrifices ever could. As Pope Benedict XVI said about the Sanhedrin and its high priest, "Only a theologically motivated declaration from the high priest, spoken with the authority of his office, could dispel their doubts and prepare them in principle for such a momentous decision."[31]

---

[28] John 11:47.
[29] John 11:50–51.
[30] Heb. 10:4.
[31] Benedict XVI, *Jesus of Nazareth*, pt. 2, *Holy Week* (San Francisco: Ignatius Press, 2011), 171–172.

Fr. Francis Canavan, S.J., puts all of this in a wider perspective:

> If sin means nothing, neither does salvation; we do not need to be saved from a ship that isn't sinking. However, Jesus's crucifixion tells us the ship is sinking. God became man to save us from our sins. It is in this sinful world into which Christ came to save us—not by taking us out of this world; our salvation is accomplished here, in the world as it is.[32]

The importance of the Crucifixion was also stressed by St. Edith Stein, a convert from Judaism, who spoke of "the science of the Cross." One could even say, in the words of Roy Schoeman, that "Christianity not only *has* a theology of suffering, but that Christianity *is* a theology of suffering."[33] This description might explain why the Shroud of Turin, with its image of a severely wounded person, has received so much attention, adoration, and devotion from Christians.

But there is more to the good news. The Crucifixion is not the end of the story—the Resurrection is. Because of the Resurrection, we know the Crucifixion achieved its intended purpose. The Resurrection and the Ascension also mean, of course, that there are no remnants of Jesus' body to be found anywhere on earth. The tomb was empty! No person, no church, no institution has primary relics of Jesus' body. If authentic, then the Shroud would be a secondary relic, meaning that it touched Christ's body and would likely constitute the only visible thing we have left of Him.

---

[32] Francis Canavan, S.J., *Fun Is Not Enough: The Complete Catholic Eye Columns* (Saint Louis: En Route Books and Media, 2018), 133.

[33] Roy Schoeman, *Salvation Is from the Jews*, 150.

The bottom line is that the Bible gives more details about the Resurrection than about the Crucifixion, without denying that the latter was necessary for the former. St. John reports:

> Peter then came out with the other disciple, and they went toward the tomb. They both ran, but the other disciple outran Peter and reached the tomb first; and stooping to look in, he saw the linen cloths lying there, but he did not go in. Then Simon Peter came, following him, and went into the tomb; he saw the linen cloths lying, and the napkin, which had been on his head, not lying with the linen cloths but rolled up in a place by itself.[34]

What We Know about Roman Execution

Until its abolishment by Constantine in 337 (replaced with hanging), crucifixion was widely practiced by many peoples across the Roman Empire.[35] It was not new to or reserved for Christ, as we know from the fact that two thieves suffered the same death as our Lord. Though the method of execution was already public and torturous, scourging commonly preceded all executions, even crucifixion. While the Mosaic law limited floggings to forty strokes,[36] the Romans imposed no such restraints, other than keeping the victim alive. The punishment was intended to cause a slow death with maximum pain and suffering.[37]

---

[34] John 20:3–7.
[35] Aurelius Victor, *De Caesaribus* 41.4.
[36] Deut. 25:3.
[37] William D. Edwards, Wesley J. Gabel, and Floyd E. Hosmer, "On the Physical Death of Jesus Christ," *JAMA* 255, no. 11 (March 21, 1986): 1455–1463, https://doi.org/10.1001/jama.1986.033 70110077025.

The instrument of scourging was the dreaded Roman scourging whip, or flagellum, the thongs of which had sharp pieces of metal or bone attached at a short distance from the tips. The Shroud of Turin reveals more than 120 scourging wounds over victim's body, most notably on his back, which indicates that he was bound with his face to a column and his arms above his head. If each flagellum had only two thongs, he must have received at least sixty strokes. Two of the flogging guards, one standing on either side of the victim, applied these strokes alternately and mercilessly.[38]

Closer analysis of the Shroud of Turin shows us that the face of the victim is covered with many bloodstains, especially on the right side, where blood vessels had been ruptured. This is most likely the result of trauma to the head. It is also an indication that the victim could have been wearing a crown of thorns. If true, then the shroud we are dealing with here is the shroud not just of any victim but of the one who was crowned with thorns.

According to three of the four Gospels, a woven crown of thorns was placed on Jesus' head during the events leading up to His Crucifixion.[39] It is not clear whether this was a regular part of crucifixion. As R. W. Hynek observes, "There is no record in history of a crown of thorns being given to anyone under sentence of death except Our Lord Himself."[40] Scripture ascribes the added torture and humiliation to the soldiers' mockery of Jesus

---

[38] The scourging of Jesus is mentioned in John 19:1, Mark 15:15, and Matthew 27:26. There is a comparable account in Luke 22:63–65.

[39] Matt. 27:29; Mark 15:17; John 19:2, 5.

[40] R. W. Hynek, *The True Likeness* (London: Sheed & Ward, 1951), 93.

as the "King of the Jews."[41] Historian Thomas De Wesselow puts it this way: "Historically, we know of only one Roman Jew who was crucified wearing a crown of thorns: Jesus. The implication is that the Shroud is the very cloth in which Jesus was wrapped for burial."[42]

Most images and paintings of the Crucifixion depict Jesus as the "King of the Jews" with a circular crown of thorns on His head, but was it really a *crown* of thorns, as popularly portrayed to us? Perhaps not. Judging from the markings on the head of the man in the Shroud, the "crown" more likely took the shape of a helmet-like head covering, known at the time as a *pileus*. Confirming the data gathered from the Shroud, a fifth-century account of the Crucifixion from St. Vincent of Lérins narrates: "They placed on his head a crown of thorns; it was, in fact, in the shape of a pileus, so that it touched and covered his head in every part."[43] The saint speculates that the soldiers struck Christ's head in order to drive the thorns of the head cap into His skull. The skullcap was further secured with a strap beneath the chin. While artists' depictions align with our notion of a regal crown, Christ's reality was even more torturous than we imagined.

After all this torture, the condemned then had to carry his cross to the place of crucifixion, where Roman soldiers would carry out the execution in gruesome and creative manners. The Romano-Jewish historian Josephus confirms the soldiers' cruel ingenuity, saying that in the siege of Jerusalem, they nailed their

---

[41] Matt. 27:11; Mark 15:2; Luke 23:3; John 18:33.

[42] Thomas De Wesselow, *The Sign: The Shroud of Turin and the Secret of the Resurrection* (London: Viking, 2012), 132.

[43] Vincent of Lérins, *Sermo in Parasceve*, quoted in Pierre Barbet, *A Doctor at Calvary* (New York: Image Books, 1963), 85.

victims to their crosses in varying ways.[44] The Roman philosopher Seneca the Younger similarly recounts, "I see crosses there, not just of one kind but made in many different ways: some have their victims with head down to the ground; some impale their private parts; others stretch out their arms on the gibbet."[45]

The shape of the gibbet could be simple: only one vertical stake. However, the construction could also be more elaborate with an extra horizontal stake. Sometimes, this cross-piece was placed at the top of the gibbet, thus creating the shape of a *T*, or capital Tau in Greek, known to many of us as the "Tau cross," which was the shape very dear to St. Francis of Assisi. At other times, the crossbeam was placed just below the top. This is the image many Christian artists have used in their paintings.

Nevertheless, the most ancient image of a Roman crucifixion we have shows the crucified victim on a T-shaped cross. We find this image in a graffito, a drawing painted on a wall, that was discovered in Puteoli, dating as far back as the first century or early second century AD.[46] Then there is the Alexamenos graffito, meant to be a mockery, representing the crucifixion of a donkey-headed man on a T-shaped cross. It was carved in plaster on a wall in Rome during the first century AD.[47]

We are so used to picturing Jesus carrying the entire Cross in its traditional form that we can hardly imagine that the victims

---

[44] Josephus, *The Jewish War* 5.11.1.

[45] Seneca, "To Marcia on Consolation," in *Moral Essays*, trans. John W. Basore (Cambridge, MA: Harvard University Press, 1946), 2:69.

[46] John Granger Cook, "Crucifixion as Spectacle in Roman Campania," *Novum Testamentum* 54, no. 1 (2012): 60, 92–98.

[47] Charles William King, *The Gnostics and Their Remains: Ancient and Medieval* (1887; Scotts Valley, CA: Createspace, 2015), 203.

of crucifixion carried only the crossbeam, which, judging from archaeological studies, is more likely to be the case. The soldiers had their victims carry the horizontal crossbeam, the *patibulum*, to the crucifixion site, where it was hoisted onto an upright post, called the *stipe*. From the Roman historian Tacitus, we learn that these stipes were secured in the ground and thus made up permanent crucifixion sites within or around the city.[48]

This study makes it more likely that Jesus carried only a crossbeam on His shoulders, and the Shroud of Turin testifies to it, too. It shows bloodstains from many wounds on the two shoulder blades. The two distinct wounded areas on the upper back make it very likely that the victim had carried only the crossbeam and not the entire cross.

At the place of execution, a group of four Roman soldiers, known as a *quaternion*, working under the command of a centurion, would affix the victim to the cross. In images of the Crucifixion, Christ is traditionally depicted with His hands and feet nailed to the Cross, but the Romans likely employed a more structurally viable tactic. True, most translations of John 20:25 state that Jesus' wounds were "in his hands," but the original Greek may be understood as any part of the arm below the elbow. Had the biblical writer the express intention of referring to the hand, he likely would have added another word to specify it.[49]

It is much more likely that the nails were inserted into the wrist, and as a matter of fact, that is what the Shroud of Turin shows. The victim was held to the cross by two nails, one in each wrist. His executioners knew then, as scientists know now, that in this position, the lungs would soon struggle for oxygen. Because

---

[48] Tacitus, *Annals* 2.32.2.
[49] Cf. the original Greek of Homer, *Iliad* 20.478–480.

the victim hung only by his wrists, with his arms outstretched, his expanded ribcage was forced to remain in the position of inspiration, making it almost impossible for the victim to exhale. His oxygen levels would decrease, while the level of carbon dioxide would increase dangerously. We will revisit this later.

It is believed that when the victim could no longer lift himself to breathe properly, he would die within a few minutes. The executioners knew how to prolong this terrible ordeal, however, by driving a nail through the victim's feet. Going by the image on the Shroud of Turin, the left foot was crossed in front of the right. Thanks to this kind of support for the feet, the victim's arms and ribcage experienced some relief from the enormous pressure of bearing the weight of the entire body.

It is not quite clear how the nail in the foot was placed, however, or whether there was a standard method for it at all. An archaeological study from 1968 lends itself to the theory that the feet of crucified persons were nailed to the cross horizontally through the heel, as opposed to vertically through the top of the foot. In this study, archaeologists discovered a first-century victim crucified in Jerusalem whose heel bone had been driven through horizontally.[50] The nail was relatively short (4.53 inches), and its end was bent, suggesting that it had struck a knot in the wooden beam. This evidence, together with the unusual entrance angle of the nail, suggests that the feet were nailed to opposite sides of the stipe.[51] Had the Shroud not depicted otherwise, the popular

---

[50] Joseph Zias and Eliezer Sekeles, "The Crucified Man from Giv'at ha-Mivtar: A Reappraisal," *Israel Exploration Journal* 35, no. 1 (1985): 22–27.

[51] David W. Chapman, *Ancient Jewish and Christian Perceptions of Crucifixion* (Tübingen: Mohr Siebeck, 2008), 86–89.

image of Christ on the Cross, with His overlapping feet secured by a single nail, may have been modified yet again.

Obviously, crucifixion is a cruel and barbaric form of execution. The Roman statesman and writer Marcus Tullius Cicero referred to it as "the most cruel and atrocious of punishments,"[52] yet it was a very common practice in the Roman Empire. It is believed that Emperor Constantine the Great, being a Christian himself, abolished its practice out of reverence for Christ.

The Jesus of History

If the Shroud of Turin is indeed the Shroud of Jesus, then this cloth ties Jesus to the reality of history. The Jesus of history is essential to Christianity. If He did not really die on the Cross, then He did not redeem humanity. If His Cross is a hoax, then the whole economy of redemption and salvation falls apart, for there is no light of Easter morning without the darkness of Good Friday afternoon.

Very often nowadays, we hear that "the Jesus of history" is not the same as "the Christ of faith." Whatever this distinction is worth, it creates a dangerous and false separation between what we know through reason about Jesus of Nazareth and what we know through faith about Jesus the Son of God. This division wrongly suggests that science sides with reason, while faith opposes it. Instead, as we discussed earlier, there is as much reason in faith as there is in science.

The so-called historical Jesus is only a product of a recent methodology: the method of modern historical analysis. Methods tend to change over time, however, and besides, they create only

[52] Cicero, *Against Verres* 2.5.165.

a hypothetical reconstruction of the life of Jesus. As a matter of fact, the Christ of faith is deeply rooted in the Jesus of history; he could only become the Christ of faith based on the person and life of Jesus as found in history.

Most notably in the past century, some theologians began to create drastically different portrayals of Jesus. They painted Him in various exclusive, often mutually contradictory ways: as an anti-Roman revolutionary, as the liberator of the poor, as a meek moral teacher, as a visionary, as an immigrant, as a radical or political activist, and so on. But as Pope Benedict XVI said in one of his sermons about these portrayals, "They are much more like photographs of their authors and the ideals they hold."[53] Nowadays, we could say that they are more like "selfies" of their authors. Their makers eliminate anything about Jesus that does not fit their own beliefs—and then they falsely declare their portrayal "the Jesus of history."

Ultimately, that which matters most is that Jesus is the Son of God. The rest of our theology flows from this understanding. This means that the Jesus of the Crucifixion is not the final figure of the story, that the Jesus of the Resurrection plays a more pivotal role. Obviously, holding Jesus as the Son of God and professing the theological truths that stem from it represent the boundary where the role of science ends, as we will discuss more extensively later in this book.

Particularly relevant for our discussion of the Shroud of Turin is the fact that the disciples found an empty, or *nearly* empty tomb. The Gospel of Luke offers a few details: "Peter rose and ran to the

---

[53] Pope Benedict XVI, *Jesus of Nazareth: From the Baptism in the Jordan to the Transfiguration* (San Francisco: Ignatius Press, 2008), xii.

tomb; stooping and looking in, he saw the linen cloths by themselves; and he went home wondering at what had happened."[54]
The Gospel of John, however, gives a more comprehensive version: "Then Simon Peter came, following him [John the Apostle],
and went into the tomb; he saw the linen cloths lying, and the
napkin, which had been on his head, not lying with the linen
cloths but rolled up in a place by itself."[55] It is a rather detailed
description. Some say the details mainly tried to emphasize that
the grave had not been robbed, but there must be more to it.

What is quite telling in St. John's description is his reference
to a head covering as well as burial cloths. Always attentive to
detail in his Gospel, St. John speaks of burial cloths in the plural.
These cloths were part of a normal Jewish burial, as St. John
specifies, "They took the body of Jesus, and bound it in linen
cloths with the spices, as is the burial custom of the Jews."[56] The
main burial cloth, the shroud, was wrapped around the body; the
head cloth, or *sudarium*, covered the face like a veil; and the other
cloths, which were more like strips or bandages, bound the dead
person's jaw, arms, and legs until rigor mortis set in. St. Luke,
too, records that Jesus' body was "wrapped in a linen shroud
[*sindoni*],"[57] and that after the Resurrection, Peter "saw the linen
cloths [*othonia*] by themselves" in the tomb.[58] Furthermore, it is
worth noting how St. John had previously described the burial
of Lazarus: "The dead man came out, his hands and feet bound
with bandages, and his face wrapped with a cloth."[59]

[54] Luke 24:12.
[55] John 20:6–7.
[56] John 19:40.
[57] Luke 23:53.
[58] Luke 24:12.
[59] John 11:44.

It is reasonable to assume that these linen cloths ("strips," "wrappings," "bandages," or "bands," depending on the translation) included what we now know as the Shroud of Turin. Why are these cloths so important to us? Since the tomb was empty, the followers of Jesus, the first Christians, had nothing physically left of Him but these cloths. It shouldn't surprise us, then, that these burial cloths were cherished relics handed on to other Christians for centuries, even millennia. They must have been priceless treasures with strong emotional significance that linked Jesus to human history and to the very event by which He redeemed mankind.

The Jesus of history is a vital part of Christianity. Almost immediately after the Crucifixion, however, some Christians flatly denied that Jesus had become part of our human history. For them, the divinity of Jesus was possible only at the cost of His humanity. The Church strongly condemned this heresy, called Docetism, which, although acknowledging Jesus as the Son of God, erroneously rejected His human nature.

The former claim of Jesus' divinity was nothing new. The Christian belief that Jesus was not only the Messiah but also the Son of God can be found throughout the New Testament. It is very prevalent in John's Gospel, which was written after the other Gospels; but even in Mark's, which was the first of the four to be written, we find this belief repeatedly proclaimed. For instance, when Jesus was baptized by John the Baptist, Mark narrates, "A voice came from heaven, 'Thou art my beloved Son; with thee I am well pleased.'"[60] The Transfiguration provides another example: "A voice came out of the cloud, 'This is my beloved

---

[60] Mark 1:11.

Son; listen to him.'"[61] Both examples clearly dictate the divine nature of Christ as the Son of God.

The second tenet of Docetism, however, the denial of Jesus' humanity, denies a critical doctrine of the Faith and was thus deemed heretical. Docetism claimed that Jesus was in essence a pure spirit. Some believed Him to be merely a ghost, while others thought His spirit resided temporarily in the celestial form of a human body. The heresy therefore "spiritualizes" everything in Christianity and separates God from the impurities of man or of matter at all. It lets Christians remain Christian while avoiding "the scandal of the Cross" and "the scandal of the Incarnation." Most Greeks and Romans could not imagine the Creator of the universe as a baby in a manger, let alone a man nailed to a cross. In the words of St. Paul, "We preach Christ crucified, a stumbling block to Jews and folly to Gentiles."[62] A notable exception was the Greek philosopher Plato, who came to the startling conclusion that a truly righteous or just man can be found only after he is stripped of all, made to suffer, and then crucified.[63] The word that Plato uses for "crucify" means literally "to fix on a pole or a stake." Although it is not the same word that the New Testament uses, it could very well be translated as "to crucify."

Docetism was on the rise during the second generation of Christianity. Its name is derived from the Greek word *dokesis*, meaning "appearance" or "semblance," because Docetism teaches that Christ only "appeared" or "seemed" to be a man, to have been born, to have lived and suffered and died. According to

---

[61] Mark 9:7.

[62] 1 Cor. 1:23.

[63] Plato, *Republic*, trans. Paul Shorey (Loeb Classical Library, 1930), 361e–362a.

this heresy, when the apostles thought they were walking and talking with Jesus, they were actually walking and talking with a mirage or some celestial appearance of the divine Son. This mirage could not possibly have suffered real pain, meaning that His suffering on the Cross was presumably nothing but a divine stunt. He only *seemed* to suffer. The God of Docetism was not the God who, according to St. Paul, "sent forth his Son, born of woman."[64]

Perhaps St. Paul was responding to the Docetic heresy when he wrote, "For in him the whole fulness of deity dwells *bodily*,"[65] or when he said, "though he was in the form of God, [Jesus] did not count equality with God a thing to be grasped, but emptied himself, taking the form of a servant, being born in the likeness of men."[66] St. John definitely referred to the same heresy: "Many false prophets have gone out into the world. By this you know the Spirit of God: every spirit which confesses that Jesus Christ has come in the *flesh* is of God."[67]

Obviously, the Shroud of Turin would be a testimony against Docetism. If it is indeed the burial cloth of the crucified Christ, the Shroud of Turin testifies that the "Jesus of history" had to suffer and die to become the "Christ of faith." Jesus certainly was a "down-to-earth" man with a human body and full human nature. Just as there exist a Jesus of history and a Christ of faith, so there may be a Shroud of history and a Shroud of faith.

---

[64] Gal. 4:4.
[65] Col. 2:9 (italics added).
[66] Phil. 2:6–7.
[67] 1 John 4:1–2 (italics added).

3

Historical Analysis

Modern spectators during expositions of the Shroud of Turin are often critical and skeptical of what it is they are observing. Many of us nowadays are hesitant to believe that the Shroud of Turin is the Shroud of Jesus. We ask for more historical evidence. We want to find out if the Shroud did indeed come from the time of Jesus and is actually imprinted with His image. We want to trace its origin back to the death of Jesus on the Cross. Can we do so? Can we find a verifiable route that brought the Shroud of Jesus from Jerusalem to Turin?

The Route of the Shroud

Since the time of Christ, reports have been popping up about a shroud that had the imprint of a male body with all the signs of torture and crucifixion. Yet these "rumors" were so vague that historians hardly gave them any attention. They knew there had been a shroud in Turin since 1578, but it did not attract their interest much; the sixteenth century was too recent to be noteworthy. This changed when it became known that in 1357 a cloth showed up in a simple wooden church in the French village of Lirey. It bore the image the rumors and reports had described: the imprint of a crucified man.

A Catholic Scientist Champions the Shroud of Turin

Where had this cloth come from before it emerged in Turin? What do we know about the Shroud before 1578? Did it just mysteriously appear without any previous history? What had happened in the years before?

The last few decades have produced more-detailed evidence about the history of the Shroud prior to the fourteenth century. Let's trace its history as far back in time as possible. The further we go, the more open-ended the historical facts may become, but this makes them nonetheless fascinating.

In 1578, the Shroud was transferred to the Cathedral of San Giovanni Battista in Turin, Italy (hence its name "the Shroud of Turin"). There it was displayed once a year for many years and was even paraded through the streets. No one doubted its authenticity — the Shroud of Turin was considered the Shroud of Jesus. But to protect the cloth, the duration and frequency of these public displays had to be reduced more and more.

However, the question still remains: where was this Shroud before it arrived in Turin?

In March 1453, Margaret de Charny deeded the Shroud to the House of Savoy, to whom it belonged for more than five hundred years (in 1983, the Savoys bequeathed the Shroud to the Holy See). After the Shroud made several detours, at the request of the Duchess Margaret of Savoy, it was decided, on June 11, 1502, that the Shroud would no longer accompany the Savoys on their travels but would be kept in the royal chapel at Chambéry, France. It was folded in forty-eight layers and kept inside a silver container. Years later, in 1532, a fire broke out in the chapel. The nuns at Chambéry, who witnessed the event and gave a written report in 1534, attested to the miraculous preservation of the Shroud, although drops of molten silver from the cloth's container did burn through the outer corners of the folded linen.[68] These recognizable markings can still be observed on the Shroud.

Where was the Shroud before it came into the House of Savoy's possession? Thanks to a written document from Bishop Pierre d'Arcis, we know that in 1390 the Shroud was present in the French town of Lirey. The document shows that the bishop believed the Shroud to have been forged.[69] This verdict was perhaps understandable because, at the time, forgery of precious relics was rather common, and the bishop concluded that the Shroud was yet another case. Nevertheless, his verdict testifies to the fact that a burial cloth matching the description of the Shroud was indeed physically present in Lirey.

The question now is how the Shroud got there. Somehow —we don't quite know *how*—the Shroud came into the possession of a French nobleman, Geoffrey de Charny. He was the Lord of Lirey and a knight who died in the Battle of Poitiers in 1356. The first public exhibition of the Shroud, where it was shown at full length, occurred a year after his death and was sponsored by the canons of the Lirey cathedral. From then on, the news spread like wildfire. Large crowds of pilgrims came to see the cloth, believing that it carried the image of the crucified Jesus.

What happened to the Shroud before it reached France? At this point, many will cite the controversial claim that, according to carbon dating performed in 1988, the Shroud did not exist before 1260 (we will discuss this in more detail later), but historical

[68] Dorothy Crispino, "The Report of the Poor Clare Nuns: Chambéry, 1534," *Shroud Spectrum International* 1, no. 2 (March 1982): 19–27, https://www.shroud.com/pdfs/ssi02part6.pdf.

[69] Emmanuel Poulle, "Les sources de l'histoire du linceul de Turin," *Revue d'Histoire Ecclésiastique* 104, nos. 3–4 (2009): 776, https://doi.org/10.1484/J.RHE.3.215.

analysis suggests otherwise. We know that the Shroud was in Constantinople when the city was sacked during the Fourth Crusade in 1204, and there are good indications that the cloth was smuggled from there to Athens, Greece, for safety. How exactly it got there we don't quite know.

It's telling that Walter II, Duke of Athens, died at Poitiers at the same time as de Charny, who had been wanting to construct a chapel to preserve the Shroud. This might suggest that Walter had given it to him in 1345 after returning from England. But that's speculation. What we do know is that the Shroud stayed in Athens until 1225. We also know that in 1205, Othon IV de la Roche had established the Duchy of Athens, taking the Shroud with him from Constantinople to Athens.[70]

Unfortunately, we do not know how the Shroud went from Athens to France. The knights of the Fourth Crusade, coming from France and Venice, may have played an important role in its transportation. A letter rediscovered in the archive of the Abbey of Santa Caterina a Formiello, located in Naples, suggests a connection. In this letter, dated August 1205, Theodore Comnenus Ducas asked Pope Innocent III for the crusaders to return the Shroud, which had been stolen from Constantinople in 1204 and taken to France. The letter states, "The Venetians partitioned the treasures of gold, silver, and ivory while the French did the same with the relics of the saints and the most sacred of all, the linen in which our Lord Jesus Christ was wrapped after his death and before the resurrection."[71] This seems to indicate that the

[70] A. S. Barnes, *The Holy Shroud of Turin* (London: Burns, Oates & Washbourne, 1934), 54–55.

[71] Pasquale Rinaldi, "Un documento probante sulla localizzazione in Atene della Santa Sindone dopo il saccheggio di Costantinopoli," in Lamberto Coppini and Francesco Cavazzuti, eds.,

Shroud had ended up in the hands of the crusaders, more specifically the Knights Templar.

We now enter a time frame in which the Shroud seemed to vanish from history. Writing in *L'Osservatore Romano*, the Vatican newspaper, on April 15, 2009, Barbara Frale, a researcher in the Vatican archives, described that what happened during that time has always puzzled historians. After the Shroud had disappeared in the sack of Constantinople in 1204, it did not surface again until the middle of the fourteenth century.

The Shroud did not vanish entirely during this "dark" period, however. Frale discovered a trial of the Knights Templar, including a document detailing the initiation of a young Frenchman in 1287. The man, Arnaut Sabbatier, testified that he was taken to "a secret place to which only the brothers of the Temple had access."[72] There he was shown "a long linen cloth on which was impressed the figure of a man" and was told to venerate it by kissing the feet three times.[73] Apparently, the Shroud had not gotten completely lost in the trails of the Crusades.

What happened to the Shroud between 1204, when Constantinople was sacked, and 1150? It is up for discussion, but we do know that the Shroud was on display until 1204 in a church in Constantinople called St. Mary of Blachernae (the remains of which still exist). Robert de Clari, one of the knights who participated in the sacking of Constantinople, left a detailed

---

La Sindone, scienza e fede (Bologna: Editrice CLUEB, 1983), 109–113.

[72] Quoted and translated in Tito Edwards, "Vatican: Knights Templar Hid the Shroud of Turin," *American Catholic*, April 5, 2009.

[73] Barbara Frale, *The Templars: The Secret History Revealed* (Dunboyne, Ireland: Maverick House, 2009), 116.

letter, dated 1203, of what he had seen: "There was another of the churches which they called My Lady Saint Mary of Blachernae, where was kept the sydoines [linens] in which Our Lord had been wrapped, which stood up straight every Friday so that the features of Our Lord could be plainly seen there."[74] Apparently, the Shroud was unfolded and lifted during display every week.

We also know that around 1150, the emperor in Constantinople had shown the Shroud to a group of Hungarian dignitaries, one of whom made a sketch of it. His drawing clearly renders those famous four holes in an L-shape caused by the Shroud's first fire. This picture ended up in a collection of medieval manuscripts, dated to the late twelfth to early thirteenth centuries, called the *Pray Codex*.

The late geneticist and Nobel laureate Jérôme Lejeune, who not only discovered the chromosomal basis of Down syndrome but also enthusiastically studied ancient manuscripts, was granted a rare private viewing of the *Pray Codex* in Budapest's National Széchényi Library in 1993. He noticed remarkable similarities with the Shroud of Turin: in both images, Jesus is shown entirely naked, with His arms on His pelvis and both of His thumbs retracted, with only four fingers visible on each hand. The fabric in the illustration shows a herringbone pattern, which is known from the Shroud of Turin. Finally, the image shows four tiny circles that look like a letter *L*. These match the marks on the Shroud caused by fire.

To go even further back, there are indications that the Shroud came to Constantinople in 944. What we know with certainty

---

[74] Edward N. Stone, ed. and trans., *Three Old French Chronicles of the Crusades* (Seattle: University of Washington Publications in Social Sciences, 1939), chap. 92.

is that, on August 15, 944, the so-called Image of Edessa came to the imperial capital Constantinople from Edessa in Muslim territory (today's Sanliurfa in Turkey). The writings of Arab historians verify that the city's emir had accepted a large sum of money from the Byzantine emperor in exchange for the Image.

But how do we know the cloth did arrive in Constantinople (which later became Istanbul after the Ottomans took over)? Thanks to a Rome classicist, Gino Zaninotto, we have access to a sermon from the Vatican Archives delivered by the archdeacon and referendary of Hagia Sophia, in the year 944. In the sermon, dated August 16, Archdeacon Gregory confirms the arrival of the Image of Edessa in Constantinople only one day before, thereby providing further reliable data as to its whereabouts.[75]

The problem, though, is determining whether this cloth of Edessa is the same as the Shroud of Turin, as the cloth is known to have portrayed only a face, while the Shroud famously depicts an entire body. The historian Ian Wilson makes a strong case for equating the two,[76] explaining that the cloth of Edessa is the Shroud of Turin folded in four. Being transported in an enclosed frame, viewers naturally would have seen only the face, while the rest of the image remained hidden.[77]

The Vatican Library's *Codex Vossianus Latinus* seems to support Wilson's theory in its eighth-century account of "a cloth on which one can see not only a face but the whole body."[78] In

---

[75] *Codex Vaticanus Graecus* 511; *Codex Vossianus Latinus* Q69.

[76] Ian Wilson, *The Shroud of Turin: Burial Cloth of Jesus?* (Garden City, NY: Image Books, 1979).

[77] Ian Wilson, *The Shroud: Fresh Light on the 2000-Year-Old Mystery* (New York: Bantam Books, 2011).

[78] *Codex Vossianus Latinus* Q69; Vatican Library, Codex 5696, fol. 35.

addition to this evidence, there exist other manuscripts testifying that the Edessa cloth included a full-body image. The source of these manuscripts was likely a Syriac text that existed before 769.[79] Eighth-century bishop Andrew of Crete describes the Image of Edessa as "the imprint ... of the bodily appearance" of Christ, which once again proposes that the cloth did not portray only a face.[80]

Even in the sixth-century *Acts of Thaddaeus*, the cloth is called a *tetradiplon*—a cloth doubled in four—meaning that it was folded twice and then fourfold. Remarkably, due to a 1978 "raking light test," we can confirm that the Shroud of Turin has the exact same folding pattern as a tetradiplon. John Jackson's test used angled light and high magnification to reveal the folding marks on the Shroud, which confirmed that they lined up exactly with the predicted pattern.[81] Oddly enough, the term tetradiplon is used so infrequently in Greek text that scholars can pinpoint its use to only two occasions—both of which refer to the Image of Edessa. These instances suggest that viewers of the cloth in these early centuries may have known that it depicted more than just a face.

What happened to the Shroud between 944 and the first century? How did the cloth get to Edessa? The early Christian historian Eusebius (260–340) reported that the "cloth with an

---

[79] Daniel Scavone, "Joseph of Arimathea, the Holy Grail, and the Edessa Icon," *Arthuriana* 9, no. 4 (1999): 18.

[80] Daniel Scavone, "A Review of Recent Scholarly Literature on the Historical Documents Pertaining to the Turin Shroud and the Edessa Icon," Proceedings of the Worldwide Congress "Sindone 2000," Orvieto, Italy, 2001, 14.

[81] Ian Wilson, *The Evidence of the Shroud* (London, UK: Michael O'Mara Books, 1986), 123.

image on it," was given to the Christian King Abgar V of Edessa as early as AD 30. Obviously, this was very soon after the Crucifixion of Jesus.[82] Abgar was described as "king of the Arabs" by Tacitus, a near-contemporary source.[83] After hearing about Jesus, Abgar became a Christian. Perhaps he may be equated with the Agabus who is mentioned in Acts of the Apostles.[84]

Others have claimed that the apostle Jude Thaddeus brought the cloth from Jerusalem to Edessa, but either way, this is where the cloth remained for hundreds of years as the Image of Edessa. Unfortunately, the cloth had to be hidden when Edessa was controlled by anti-Christian rulers (Persian and Islamic), until it was recovered in 525, hidden in the wall above one of the gates of the city. A written document of Evagrius Scholasticus, a Turkish scholar, enables historians to track the physical cloth to Edessa in the year 593, referring to it as "an image of divine origin."[85]

Whether the Edessa cloth and the Shroud of Turin are the same or not, the image on the cloth must have been known to many people. Even the tenth-century Muslim historian Massoudi knew about the cloth. It is interesting to note his remark that the cloth and its image had "circulated" before its arrival at the Edessa cathedral.[86] Apparently, many must have had a chance to see the image on the cloth during that time. This might explain why we see the characteristic features of the Shroud appear on many frescos, paintings, and icons made during that time.

---

[82] Eusebius, *Church History* 1.13.5–22.

[83] Tacitus, *Annals* 12.12ff.

[84] Acts 11:27–30.

[85] Evagrius, in Jacques-Paul Migne, *Patrologia Graeca*, lxxxvi, 2, cols. 2748f.

[86] Andrew Palmer, "The Inauguration Anthem of Hagia Sophia in Edessa," *Byzantine and Modern Greek Studies* 12 (1988): 130.

A Catholic Scientist Champions the Shroud of Turin

As a matter of fact, many Byzantine Christ portraits in frescos and icons share a striking resemblance to one another. Ian Wilson summarizes some of these common characteristics: a streak across the forehead; an open square between the brows; a V-shape at the bridge of the nose; a raised right eyebrow; accentuated left and right cheeks; an enlarged left nostril; an accented line between the nose and the lower lip; a heavy line under the lower lip; a hairless area between the lower lip and the beard; a forked beard; a transverse line across the throat; heavily accented owlish eyes; and two strands of hair at the forehead.[87]

Although the Bible doesn't give us a physical description of Jesus, it is remarkable that we suddenly find images pop up in the sixth century depicting Christ as He appears on the Shroud. We find this and the other features mentioned above in various frescos, icons, and paintings. To name the most famous ones: the eighth-century *Christ Pantocrator* in the catacomb of St. Pontianus, Rome; the eleventh-century *Daphni Pantocrator*; the tenth-century Sant'Angelo in Formis fresco; the tenth-century Hagia Sophia narthex mosaic; and the eleventh-century *Christ the Merciful* mosaic in Berlin. A late eleventh-century to early twelfth-century Byzantine ivory panel, displayed in the Victoria and Albert Museum in London, shows Jesus' arms crossed at the wrists, right over left, exactly as they appear on the Shroud. It also shows Jesus lying on a double-length cloth that has a repeating pattern similar to the Image of Edessa. These examples strongly suggest that there must have been a common, original model for these rather unusual Shroud-like features. The older depictions also verify the Shroud's existence backward by almost a millennium.

[87] Wilson, *The Shroud of Turin: Burial Cloth of Jesus?*, 141.

This leaves us with the last question: What happened to the Shroud during the first decades of Christianity? The Gospels offer no information beyond the discovery of the linens in the tomb. Could the Shroud have been thrown away? Considering its significance, this theory is highly unlikely, yet the Shroud left no clear trace behind during this period. The more reasonable presumption is that it had to be hidden carefully during the many Roman persecutions of the first three centuries AD. These persecutions were so cruel, ingenious, and well organized that they would have made Communist regimes envious. Naturally, one can speculate that the Christians had to come up with equally ingenious ways to hide their treasures.

Yet there must have been a direct connection between the images on the burial cloth and the first Christians, who had witnessed Jesus' Crucifixion and Resurrection. Some even suggest that St. Paul was well acquainted with what we know now as the Shroud of Turin. They quote him from his Second Letter to Timothy: "When you come, bring the cloak that I left with Carpus at Troas, also the books, and above all the parchments."[88] Is this connection pure speculation? Perhaps not. The Greek word for "cloak" (*phelonion*) could also translate as "garment." The word is used nowadays for a liturgical vestment worn by priests of the Eastern Christian tradition. Because it is mentioned before referring to the books and parchments, it must have been more valuable than a cloak.

According to legend, the Shroud was secretly carried from Judea in AD 30 or 33 to Edessa, Turkey. Perhaps the burial cloth of Jesus was even moved for a while into the catacombs of Rome around AD 65. That's not so unlikely, for highly valued relics were often hidden in catacombs to keep them from being destroyed

---

[88] 2 Timothy 4:13.

by enemies of Christians in the time of persecution. The burial Shroud of Jesus would certainly be number one on that list of relics. The catacombs of Rome were a place no one would expect the Shroud to be hidden. As a matter of fact, frescoes found in the catacombs show the face as if the Shroud was their model.

It should certainly not surprise us that the first Christians held everything connected to Jesus in high esteem—not only the words He spoke, but also the items He touched. They must have treasured them and shared them with their fellow Christians. The Shroud of Jesus would certainly not be an exception. This does not necessarily mean, of course, that the Shroud of Turin is the burial cloth of Jesus, but it would explain why the cloth of Jesus' burial was so faithfully handed on through generations of Christians. It was what they considered a relic of utmost divine importance.

Let's round up this long story from the past. We end up with a long trail of historical facts along the route of the Shroud. There are some rather weak links in the chain, but written documents that directly reference the cloth or its image provide solid historical markers along the way.

The Facts of History

Historians work with historical facts. Their facts usually come from witnesses, records, archives, and, more recently, photographs, videos, and the like. It is always possible to attack the witnesses or records behind certain historical facts, as has been shamefully done with the Holocaust. But nowadays, it has almost become a new fashion to create "fake news." It is hard to keep the ideal of truth, and nothing but the truth, alive in such an environment.

In the previous section, I mentioned several historical facts about the Shroud of Turin. Not surprisingly, some of them have been questioned by historians. Yet historical facts are important to reconstruct history. If Jesus was not crucified under Pontius Pilate, for instance, and that presumed fact turned out to be wrong—or more accurately, it turned out *not* to be a historical fact—then that would be the end of the Jesus story. Without the Crucifixion, there is no Resurrection.

The problem at hand is how to verify that historical facts are indeed facts. The Crucifixion of Jesus, for instance, is only a fact if Jesus was "in fact" crucified at a certain time and place. Facts are not things you can touch, see, hear, or bump into. So, we cannot take our historical facts into a laboratory to test them, as we can with material objects. Instead, we need witnesses and historical records to validate any historical claim. Something similar can be said about the Shroud of Turin. The fact that the Shroud of Turin is the same as the cloth containing the Image of Edessa is a historical fact only if we have records and witnesses to "prove" that this is the case; otherwise, it is not a fact and instead may turn out to be mere fiction.

But that's not where the problem ends. Historical facts—actually, any kind of facts—come with *interpretation*. This means that historical facts are interpretations of events in history. It's through interpretation that historical *events* are transformed into historical *facts*. When speaking of facts, we claim much more than what we observe because facts inevitably come with interpretation. What this entails is that a lack of *interpretation* leads to a lack of *information*. The more interpretation we inject into a fact, the more information the fact provides, but also the more evidence is needed to confirm it.

Let's take the following simple example. When we describe a certain event taking place in the sky by saying, "Those are moving *spots*," we do express a fact, but it contains pretty empty information. It's "safe" and easy to confirm but doesn't add much to our knowledge. When we say, however, "Those are flying *birds*," we state a fact that includes additional information—and therefore we need to come up with more evidence to support it. When we say, "Those are migrating *geese*," we inflate our information even further. As you can see, all three interpretations concern the same event taking place in the sky, but the facts are very different.

Which of the three statements is true and qualifies as a fact? Perhaps none of them, or one of them, but it is also possible that all three of them are true. If those things in the sky are geese, then they are also birds, and even moving spots. A more general fact can include more specific facts. However, if you decide to go for the presumably "safest" information, you take the least risk of being inaccurate, but you do not have much to tell the world.

This comparison may be helpful to understand the problem of historical analysis surrounding the Shroud of Turin. Most historians tend to take on a "scientific" attitude, which they borrowed from their colleagues in the natural sciences. They like to go for facts with the safest kind of information—that is, facts with minimal informational content and the least amount of interpretation, comparable to the claim of "moving spots." This approach, however, often leads to rather empty information, out of fear that there is not enough evidence to support any further claims. Historians who take this approach don't allow themselves to go for facts with a richer informational content because they feel held back by a lack of additional supporting records or witnesses. They want to be scientifically and politically "correct" at all times.

There is nothing wrong with being cautious and critical about historical claims; however, we ought to recognize the cost: it may deprive us of important informational content. Why do we have to go for facts with minimal information over facts with more? Why would "simple" facts be better than "significant" ones?

This idea reminds me of how Occam's razor is used in science—a principle that could be paraphrased as "the simplest solution is most likely the right one." Really? For example, would explaining a hereditary characteristic by only one gene be more likely, let alone more correct, than an explanation by several genes? Too many genetic characteristics are still too often explained by assuming one gene, whereas they are actually based on a combination of genes. Many textbooks, especially those for high schools, still mention a simplistic, monogenic form of inheritance for human characteristics such as eye color, large or small earlobes, sticky or dry earwax, the ability or inability to curl the tongue (tongue rolling), and the development of certain diseases such as epilepsy, to name just a few. The simplest solution may not always be the right one, however. Very often the expression of a certain gene is regulated by others, called regulatory genes. Simplicity gone!

Taken to its extreme, the principle of Occam's razor may eventually lead to saying almost nothing about nearly everything. We may not be able to validate every detail about migrating geese, but we know enough to say that they are more than flying birds, let alone moving spots in the sky. Of course, rejecting the extreme of nearly meaningless facts does not provide us with a free pass to the other extreme, burdening our facts with extravagant claims.

A case in point for our discussion is the historical *fact* that icons and frescos were modeled after the face on the Shroud of Turin, which contrasts with claiming the opposite *fact* that their similarities are merely coincidental. Do we have enough evidence for the former claim? Probably not enough to convince every historian, but we do have quite a bit to confirm the claim. It doesn't make much sense to reject detailed information based on a rather arbitrary rule of going for the "simplest solution" in favor of a fact with nearly empty informational content.

The aim of historical analysis is not a search for completely confirmed, safe facts but rather a pursuit of meaningful, informative ones. As a matter of fact, nothing about historical facts can be completely and decisively proven, unless the fact is devoid of any informational content. As in science, historical analysis can neither completely prove nor disprove what is claimed to be a historical fact.

The Missing Facts

As we discussed already, there are a few facts missing in the sequence of events on the alleged trail that brought the Shroud from Jerusalem to Turin. This makes many historians quite nervous. To be scientifically and politically correct, they jump (almost automatically) to the conclusion that there is no connection between the Shroud of Jesus and the Shroud of Turin. End of the discussion? Not yet!

Although there are indeed some gaps in the sequence of events, that does not mean the entire sequence is unreliable. There is still reasonable evidence for the route of the Shroud from Jerusalem to Turin.

There are at least two ways to deal with this problem: one is logical; the other is philosophical. Let's start with the logical approach. Claiming that there is no evidence to support a certain historical fact amounts to proving a *universal negative* — that is, to prove that something does *not* exist. However, we have a problem here: such a proof is logically impossible.

In general, it is hard to prove the assertion of a universal negative. It's possible, for instance, to establish that there is a black swan somewhere on earth, but it is logically unwarranted to claim that there are *none* at all. If you look for X and don't find it, that doesn't prove that there is no X at all. In this case, if you don't find a record that says the Shroud was present in Greece, then you may have to wait until someone comes up with such a record. In the meantime, we cannot prove the Shroud was never in Greece.

Be aware, though, that the key word here is *universal.* You might be able to say that there is no black swan in the Franklin Park Zoo in Boston, but it is logically impossible to say there is no black swan anywhere in the universe. The latter would require a search that is potentially unending. There is always the possibility that someday we may find one.

Another way of dealing with the problem of missing facts is of a more philosophical nature. Although it's related to the issue of proving a universal negative, it has a much wider application. When there is no record that indicates that a certain event took place, the lacking creates a "gap" in a historical sequence of events. As mentioned already, missing gaps in a sequence of historical facts make most historians pretty uncomfortable. When certain historical evidence is missing, they tend to dismiss the entire sequence of events. Is there reason to do so?

In the philosophy of science, this situation is often described thus: "absence of evidence is not evidence of absence."[89] Simply put, it means that if we don't know that something exists

---

[89] This statement is usually attributed to the astrophysicist Carl Sagan, who borrowed it from the cosmologist Martin Rees, but it goes as far back as the geologist W. J. Sollas who used it as early as 1895.

(which is "absence of evidence"), it doesn't mean that it doesn't exist (which is "evidence of absence"). Evidence of absence is evidence that indicates that some proposed object or fact does not exist or hold true, although it does not confirm the negative with certainty. For instance, the fact that we have never found life other than on earth, which is "absence of evidence," does not mean that there is no life somewhere else in the universe, for that would amount to claiming "evidence of absence." The question is always whether we can detect something if it exists.

Back to the Shroud's history. When there is no historical record about a certain event, such as the Templars' holding the Shroud in their possession, does that mean this event did not happen? Certainly not. The record might have disappeared or might never have been written down in the first place. The latter proposition is very likely to be the case in any matter that relates to a time when recording and archiving were not as common as they are nowadays.

Therefore, I would like to render "absence of evidence is not evidence of absence" in a safer, more accurate way: "absence of proof isn't proof of absence." In cases of "absence of evidence," we merely classify them as unproven, but not as impossible. But let's not forget that "unproven" does not mean "false." The claim that there is no recorded evidence about the Shroud between 1204 and 1225, between being in Greece and ending up in France, does not mean that such a connection is false, only that it is unproven.

In other words, even if there are not enough records, or enough evidence, to confirm the Shroud's route from Jerusalem to Turin in detail, that doesn't mean we have to abandon the idea that there was such a route. The only case in which absence of evidence is not evidence of absence is when no attempt whatsoever has been made to obtain evidence. In the previous section, it was shown that many attempts have been made to obtain evidence for a long sequence of events connecting the Shroud of Turin to the Shroud of Jerusalem.

So we must come to the conclusion that science does not have the last word, not even in historical analysis, when it comes to the Shroud of Turin. Its analyses and conclusions at least should not contradict what faith tells us but may even confirm what we know based on faith. Religious faith may add new elements and insights that are beyond the scope of the historical analysis done by science.

4

Computer Analysis

When the Shroud was displayed in the cathedral of San Giovanni Battista in Turin in 1978, millions of people eagerly seized this opportunity to see the Shroud with their very own eyes. Many of them, however, must have been a bit disappointed about what they saw on the cloth, after having been exposed to so many impressive, colorful photos of it. In reality, the frontal and dorsal image of a body on the cloth is only vaguely visible and hardly recognizable as a human being. It is almost hidden amid burn marks, the patches, the water stains, and the creases.

Because it is one of the most venerated objects in the Roman Catholic Church, the Shroud of Turin is now safely stored in a bombproof case. It makes sense that it has been protected from exposure to the public, both now and throughout history. In the last hundred years, it has made only five public appearances. Pope Paul VI presented the Shroud in its first televised showing in 1973. Five years later, the cloth was presented again — this time in commemoration of the four hundredth anniversary of its arrival in Turin. About three million people visited the public showing during the two-month display from August 27 to October 3, 1978. In 2000, another three million visited the Shroud, and even more are expected to venerate it in the next display in 2025.

What No Eye Had Seen

The explanation for the rather sudden rise in popularity of the Shroud of Turin is rather simple. To make visible what is really shown on the cloth requires additional, and often advanced, techniques. Thanks to such techniques, we are now able to see on the Shroud what had been hidden to previous generations.

The first notable technique, photography, shone light onto many of these hidden realities. In 1898, Italian photographer Secondo Pia photographed the Shroud for the first time, raising scientific, and even popular, observation to new heights. The negatives of the photos, which reverse the light and dark values, illustrated an image much more dramatic and detailed than was previously available to the naked eye. Pia's photograph, developed into a black-and-white positive, presented a natural-looking image of the man in the Shroud, which, predictably, renewed fascination with the mysterious cloth around the world. Thirty-three years later, inspired by these advances, the Church commissioned a second, more sophisticated photographing by Giuseppe Enrie.

Much later, in 1973, physicist John Jackson and his colleague Eric Jumper of the U.S. Airforce Academy made computer scans of photographs previously taken of the Shroud. Jumper, specializing in aerodynamics, applied NASA's VP-8 Image Analyzer to the photos. This technology, used in aerospace science, analyzes differences in the brightness levels of an image to determine elevation levels, with the brighter spots revealing higher elevation and the darker ones revealing lower. By analyzing the elevation variation of the image of the Shroud, Jackson and Jumper transformed the photograph into a three-dimensional map of the body, depicting the features of the man as he appears on the cloth—not in agony, but in serene rest.[90] This serenity in a man who clearly endured extreme agony can make sense only if we look to the Scriptures, remembering that with Jesus' last words, "Father, into thy hands I commit my spirit,"[91] He completes His Passion and enters into the peace of death.

The Image Analyzer did not reveal only the man's expressions and dimensions, however. By measuring the relative darkness on the photo negatives, the Image Analyzer revealed the distance between the body and the cloth at various spots. If there was more distance between body surface and cloth, the spots appeared darker; if there was less distance, the spots appeared lighter. This study of elevation variation and relative brightness levels indicated that the cloth itself contains "distance information." In order to convey such information, the cloth must have enshrouded the figure that it portrays. In other words, the man in the Shroud had to have been wrapped by the linens at some point for the cloth to contain "distance information" at all. This discovery is bad news for those who claim that a painter had created the cloth, for how could a two-dimensional painting ever include three-dimensional information of a real body?

A 1981 summary reports the following:

> Computer image enhancement and analysis by a device known as a VP-8 image analyzer show that the image has unique, three-dimensional information encoded in it. Microchemical evaluation has indicated no evidence of any

---

[90] John P. Jackson, Eric J. Jumper, and William R. Ercoline, "Correlation of Image Intensity on the Turin Shroud with the 3-D Structure of a Human Body Shape," *Applied Optics*, 23 (1984): 2244.

[91] Luke 23:46.

spices, oils, or any biochemicals known to be produced by the body in life or in death. It is clear that there has been a direct contact of the Shroud with a body, which explains certain features such as scourge marks, as well as the blood. However, while this type of contact might explain some of the features of the torso, it is totally incapable of explaining the image of the face with the high resolution that has been amply demonstrated by photography.[92]

A more recent photographing took place in 2008, shot with high-definition cameras and aided with various computer techniques. HAL9000, a business that specializes in art photography, created a 12.8-billion-pixel image of the Shroud—an image well over a thousand times stronger than one produced by a 10-million-pixel camera. To do this, the technicians pieced together 1,600 different close-up shots of the cloth. Upon viewing the finished product, the project supervisor, Mauro Gavinelli, commented that "it [was] like looking at the shroud through a microscope."

The Shroud of Turin Research Project

Jackson and Jumper went on to form the Shroud of Turin Research Project, or STURP, made up of more than twenty of the most qualified specialists from research centers around the country, including Los Alamos National Laboratory and the Jet Propulsion Laboratory in Pasadena. The team recruited a pathologist and two photographers to aid in their research. STURP was allowed to access the Shroud directly for the duration of the project. After

---

[92] "A Summary of STURP's Conclusions" (1981), Shroud of Turin website, https://www.shroud.com/78conclu.htm.

two years of preparation, in October 1978, twenty-five special-ists visited Turin to gather many and various data samples. They spent five full days there, studying the Shroud around the clock in a room at the Royal Palace adjoining the Turin cathedral. According to descriptions given by members of the team, the specialists performed several advanced tests on the linen, including photographic floodlighting, low-power X-rays, and narrow-band ultraviolet lighting. To take samples without damaging or cutting into the cloth, the scientists drew particles from its surface using sticky tape. The STURP professionals also took apart an edge from the side and bottom of the Shroud to examine the underside and its support cloth, known as "Holland cloth."

Armed with a wealth of photo negatives, graphics, charts, and samples, the team members went back to the United States, where they used various techniques to study the composition of the Shroud better than ever before. Using X-ray fluorescence, for instance, high concentrations of iron were found in certain spots, which might indicate that they are bloodstains, since iron is a component of the hemoglobin molecule in blood.

The final paragraph of STURP's written report read:

> We can conclude for now that the Shroud image is that of a real human form of a scourged, crucified man. It is not the product of an artist. The bloodstains are composed of hemoglobin and also give a positive test for serum albumin. The image is an ongoing mystery, and until further chemical studies are made, perhaps by this group of scientists, or perhaps by some scientists in the future, the problem remains unsolved.[93]

[93] STURP scientists publicly shared their findings at a 1981 international conference in New London, Connecticut.

The Body Buried in the Shroud

STURP's discoveries made a grand media appearance in *National Geographic* magazine in June 1980. The article and its photos from STURP incited widespread interest in the Shroud, both in the academic world and in the mainstream media.[94] The Shroud was declared "one of the most perplexing enigmas of modern times." The impression remained as thirty years later, in 2010, *Time* magazine called it "The Riddle of the Ages."

To best characterize the Shroud is to see it as a negative image of the body wrapped within. Combined with other techniques, mentioned above, we can see a man lying on a cloth that was folded midway over his head to cover the other side of his body. We also can see marks from heavy injuries on the head, the arms, and on both sides. Much fluid had leaked from the wound on the left side and had streamed to the bottom of the sheet. The left wrist displays wounds, too, but because it crosses over the right, wounds on the other wrist are not exposed. The small bloodstains from both arms, however, lead us to assume that both wrists had been pierced by a nail. There is also blood around the feet, which indicates that they were pierced as well.

On both sides of the folded cloth we see the stains caused by the 1532 fire in Chambéry. The pattern of these stains tells us how the cloth had been folded at the time. Reparations had been made by stitching small pieces of cloth over the damaged areas by the Poor Clare nuns of Chambéry.

Other details of the Shroud were revealed by Vernon Miller who, in 1978, as a member of the Shroud of Turin Research

---

[94] K. F. Weaver, "Science Seeks to Solve the Mystery of the Shroud," *National Geographic* 157, no. 6 (1980): 730–753.

Project, made photographs of the cloth by using an ultraviolet filter.[95] These UV-reflection pictures showed details that no human eye had seen. The part of the cloth that showed the back of the body revealed diagonal lines that may align with the characteristic scourges caused by a Roman whip.

Obviously, there is much to be seen on the Shroud that goes unnoticed by the naked eye. In this issue, technology comes to our aid. The advances of science have given us new techniques—leading to facts and information we would not have known otherwise. They confirm what biblical analysis and historical analysis have already told us. Combined, they make a strong case for the authenticity of the Shroud of Turin.

After all this study, we must remember that science does not have the last word, even when using computer analysis, when it comes to the Shroud of Turin. Scientific findings, whatever they may be, should not contradict what faith tells us, and, contrary to popular opinion, religious faith has the ability to add to that which is beyond the scope of computer analytics, even science itself.

---

[95] V. D. Miller and S. F. Pellicori, "Ultraviolet Fluorescence Photography of the Shroud of Turin," *Journal of Biological Photography* 49, no. 3 (1981): 71–85.

5

Anatomical Analysis

The figure on the Shroud of Turin can reveal important facts about the anatomy, and perhaps physiology, of the person who was wrapped in the linen. Thanks to the techniques we discussed in the previous chapter, we are able to extract such information from the cloth better than ever before. The marks in the Shroud allow us to perform an "autopsy" (so to speak) of the man buried in the linen cloth.

Anatomical Features

There is no mistaking that the image visible on the Shroud is of a bearded male who was relatively tall and mature in age. Being nearly five foot eleven (1.65 meters), the man in the Shroud would have been about six inches taller than the average male at the time. Apparent from the many bloodstains and visible wounds, the man had undergone significant physical injury. The back of the Shroud shows markings of Roman scourging, the head displays many wounds, and there is a distinct gash in the man's left side. More detailed forensic investigation[96] reveals numerous

[96] Brooke Kaelin, "What Does Forensic Science Reveal about the Shroud of Turin?," *Forensic Science Degree* (blog), December

puncture wounds around the top and back of the man's forehead. His face had been beaten, and he likely had fallen at some point, causing swelling on his cheeks. The wound in his left wrist proves consistent with Roman crucifixion, although the right wrist is not visible. The man's shoulders and back appear swollen, further aligning with the injuries of crucifixion. Despite the many severe physical wounds, however, it is important to note that the legs of the man were not broken, as specified by John's Gospel.[97] In this analysis, we see again and again the amazing anatomical and biblical accuracy of the image on the Shroud.

With the help of sculptor Sergio Rodella, Giulio Fanti, a professor of mechanical and thermal measurements at the University of Padua, created a statue—a "3-D carbon copy," as he called it—of what the figure on the Shroud must have looked like. In Fanti's own words, "This statue is the three-dimensional representation in actual size of the Man of the Shroud, created following the precise measurements taken from the cloth in which the body of Christ was wrapped after the crucifixion."[98]

Sometimes new discoveries start with simple observations. It appears, for instance, that the right arm of the figure on the Shroud is six centimeters (2.36 inches) longer than the left one. Two researchers, the radiologist Filippo Marchisio at the Rivoli

---

31, 2015, https://www.forensicsciencedegree.org/what-does -forensic-science-reveal-about-the-shroud-of-turin/.

[97] See John 19:33.

[98] See Maria Teresa Martinengo, "Una statua restituisce le fattezze dell'uomo della Sindone" (A statue returns the features of the man of the Shroud), La Stampa, last edited June 16, 2019, http:// www.lastampa.it/2018/03/20/cronaca/una-statua-restituisce-le- fattezze-delluomo-della-sindone-hqN5guzFKnxuNbAtowgkHL/ pagina.html.

Hospital, and Pierluigi Baima Bollone, professor of forensic medicine at the University of Turin, attribute the difference to either an elbow fracture or a shoulder dislocation.[99] Both possibilities explain the elongated arm while holding consistent with potential injuries from crucifixion. However, the hypotheses of Marchisio and Bollone remain just that—hypotheses. The partial destruction of the images of the arms and shoulders from the fire of 1532 inhibit further examination.

Scientific Controversies

Anatomy especially seems to be a matter-of-fact science, but as is the case with all sciences, it is not so black and white in reality. Scientists must defend their own "facts" from the counterevidence of others and argue against the "facts" of other scientists with which they do not agree. This may not seem science-like, but it is both common and necessary in the scientific community. The "facts" or theories of scientists are not etched in stone but are subject to serious debates that may end in the discrediting of the facts. Nothing in science is definite or definitive; the assumed facts are always open to discussion and revision, and the Shroud of Turin is no exception to this rule.

Just think of this classic example. For several decades, it was believed to be a fact that human beings have forty-eight chromosomes. Nowadays, that's no longer a fact; it turns out that we have forty-six chromosomes. What seems to be a simple case of

---

[99] Diane Montagna, "New Discoveries Prove Man on Shroud of Turin Was 'Really Crucified,'" LifeSiteNews, January 11, 2019, https://www.lifesitenews.com/news/new-discoveries-prove-man-on-shroud-of-turin-was-really-crucified.

counting turned out to be not that simple — we need something to count, to begin with, and that may not be easily visible or accessible. But no matter what the technical problem is, it's not that the facts changed, but that what we thought was a fact turned out *not* to be a fact.

Controversies and disagreements about anatomical features on the Shroud of Turin are to be expected, as science never has definite conclusions. For nearly every scientist, there will be one with a different, or opposing, opinion. Here are just a few examples.

Anatomical Issues

How authentic and anatomically correct are the features on the Shroud? Drawing on his experience as a surgeon in World War I, French physician Pierre Barbet declared the anatomical conditions of the man in the Shroud authentic and the wounds consistent with those of crucified victims.[100] Barbet, who had done fifteen years of medical research on the image of the Shroud of Turin, described the physiology and pathology of the crucified man on the Shroud as "almost perfect from the anatomical point of view."[101] Despite his affirmation of authenticity, however, his opinion, given in 1950, was only the beginning of a decades-long controversy.

A second opinion came from Frederick Zugibe, professor of pathology at Columbia University Vagelos College of Physicians and Surgeons. In order to verify the anatomical conditions of a crucified person, the professor suspended himself and other volunteers from crosses and noted the physiological responses.

---

[100] Pierre Barbet, A *Doctor at Calvary* (New York: Image Books, 1963).

[101] Pierre Barbet, M.D., A *Doctor at Calvary: The Passion of Our Lord Jesus Christ as Described by a Surgeon* (Manchester, UK: Allegro Editions, 2014), 92.

In his 1998 book, Zugibe also authenticated the image on the Shroud but presented alternative judgements on various details outlined by Barbet's study.[102]

Opposing the statements of authentication made by Barbet and Zugibe, researcher Joe Nickell declared the anatomical proportions of the body unrealistic and impossible, therefore asserting that the man in the Shroud was not a real man. He pointed to the different arm lengths and the unusually small size of the forehead as evidence: the man could not have been real. As an alternative theory, Nickell proposed that the Shroud was created by an unknown Gothic artist, connecting the physical inconsistencies to popular stylistic trends of the period.[103]

The discussion surrounding these controversies can get very heated and personal. Zugibe stated candidly, "Unfortunately, the medical aspects of the Shroud-crucifixion literature are filled with a farrago of articles by unqualified individuals including surgeons, radiologists, general practitioners, psychiatrists, scientists and scholars in other areas of expertise, laymen, etc. whose conclusions were based on anecdotal, a priori speculations."[104]

Marks around the Hands

The crucifixion marks around the hands caused further controversy, as researchers questioned whether the nails were strong

---

[102] Frederick Zugibe, *The Crucifixion of Jesus: A Forensic Inquiry* (New York: M. Evans & Company, 2005), chaps. 9 and 20.

[103] Joe Nickell, "Crucifixion Evidence Debunks Turin 'Shroud,'" *Skeptical Inquirer* 42, no. 5 (2018): 7.

[104] Zugibe, *The Crucifixion of Jesus*, introduction; Frederick T. Zugibe, *Forensic and Clinical Knowledge of the Practice of Crucifixion* (Turin: International Scientific Symposium, March 2–5, 2000), http://www.crucifixion-shroud.com/Turin2000.htm.

enough to bear the weight of a grown man. Barbet conducted a study of the matter by inserting nails into the palms of fresh cadavers. He observed that at a weight of eighty-eight pounds the flesh tore through to the fingers, thus concluding that the weight of a nearly six-foot-tall man undoubtedly would not be able to be suspended by a nail inserted into each hand. Further proving the impossibility, Barbet's mathematical calculations revealed that when the arms are suspended at an angle of sixty-five degrees, the hands experience a pull greater than the weight of the body.[105] As Barbet later notes, however, the nail wounds on the man in the Shroud were not located in the palms but instead where the wrist meets the hand.

Often in artwork, statues, and crucifixes, the wounds in Jesus' hands are placed in the middle of the *palm* of the hand. As shown by Barbet, and argued by others, this placement is very unlikely because a nail through the palm would not be sufficient to hold a person's weight on a cross; the nail would tear through the hand. This led many to believe that the placement of the nails during crucifixion had to be in the *wrist*.

Don't confuse the wrist with the place where most people wear their wristwatch. Wristwatches are usually worn on the anatomical forearm, not on one's anatomical wrist. When medical experts claim that the nails of Jesus' Crucifixion must have been driven through His wrists, they refer to the anatomical wrist in the "heel" of the hand. The wrist connects the two forearm bones with the metacarpal bones located between the phalanges of the fingers and the carpal bones of the wrist.

The wrist consists of two rows of four small bones, known as the carpal bones. These eight bones of the wrist are located in the

---

[105] Barbet, *A Doctor at Calvary* (Allegro), 96.

heel of the hand, at the part of the palm closest to the forearm. This location would allow the nails to support the weight of an adult man because the ligaments that join the eight wrist bones are thicker and stronger than those that connect the bones of the palm (the metacarpal bones).

The question then becomes: Where in the wrist did the nail enter? It is unlikely that it was placed in the palms, as popularly depicted in religious art, due to the placement of the nail wound on the man in the Shroud. Had the nail been inserted as high as the middle palm, it would not have been able to exit at the location shown in the Shroud. Alternatively, there are two reasonable options: a place on the thumb side (or radial) of the wrist (the so-called Destot's space bounded by four bones) or a place on the little finger (the ulnar) side of the wrist (called the Z-area, bounded by four other carpal bones). Yet here the controversy starts again.

Barbet argued for the placement in the thumb side of the wrist, using the missing thumb on the Shroud as evidence. As he explains in his defense, injury to the median nerve caused by the nail would make the thumb involuntarily retract into the palm of the hand. Barbet demonstrated the reaction by driving a nail through Destot's space in an amputated hand.

That's when Zugibe retorted: "Having M.S. and Ph.D. degrees in human anatomy, I immediately realized that Barbet [had] made a very serious error because the space bounded by these four bones are located on the little finger (ulnar) side of the wrist not on the thumb (radial) side as is depicted on the Shroud!"[106] Zugibe considers the Z-area on the ulnar side more likely than the Destot's space because it's more anatomically consistent with the

[106] Zugibe, *Forensic and Clinical Knowledge.*

evidence on the Shroud. Zugibe also attacked Barbet's argument of the missing thumb because, in his own words, "the median nerve does not pass through Destot's space and even if it did and was injured, there would be no flexion of the thumb." Besides, he notes, "Barbet was obviously striking the ulnar nerve and not the median nerve when he drove a nail through Destot's space on the amputated hand."[107]

To explain the "missing thumbs" in the Shroud, Zugibe points out that even in life, when relaxed, the thumb is located slightly to the side and in front of the index finger. The positioning remains the same after death. Zugibe notes that deceased persons are wrapped tightly, in a manner in which the thumb nearly always contracts into the palm. In the case of the man in the Shroud, it is most likely that the two hands were folded together with the thumbs interlocking beneath the palms—a clear reason for their lack of visibility.

Is this an earth-shaking controversy? For most people, it probably is not. Yet it shows again how even experts disagree on rather basic scientific issues. Sometimes there isn't even a general agreement about the anatomical facts.

Marks on the Feet

The crucifixion marks on the feet have also caused much debate. In 2007, archaeologists uncovered the remains of a crucified Roman whose *heels* displayed the nail wounds, rather than the tops of the feet, as shown on the Shroud. This discovery, in conjunction with similar evidence demonstrated by other crucified victims, shows a lack of consistency in the Roman method of crucifixion. Nickell notes the difference between the foot wounds, while

[107] Ibid.

also pointing out the puzzling lack of wrist wounds on the other crucifixion victims.[108]

These findings contradict the conclusions many other scientists have come to regarding the placement of the nails in the feet. For example, the initial conclusions of the crucifixion victim discovered in Jerusalem had to be revisited and amended. In revisiting the case, Hebrew University anatomy researcher Nicu Haas stated that "[the] feet were joined almost parallel, both transfixed by the same nail at the heels, with the legs adjacent."[109]

A second reassessment came in 1985 from Joe Zias, a curator of the Israel Department of Antiquities and Museums, and Eliezer Sekeles, from the Hadassah Medical Center. The two claimed that Haas's conclusions had been erroneous on multiple accounts. "The nail was shorter than Haas had reported and thus would not have been long enough to pierce two heel bones and the wood."[110] The researchers further recounted that "[pieces] of bone had been misidentified," "[there] was no bone from a second heel," and that "[some] of the bone fragments were from another individual" altogether.[111] All this is to say that, apparently, even "simple" anatomical evidence may not be so simple after all. Controversies abound.

The Cause of Death

There is also much debate about the cause of death during crucifixion. The most common explanation is that crucified victims

[108] Nickell, "Crucifixion Evidence Debunks," 7.
[109] Nicu Haas, "Anthropological Observations on the Skeletal Remains from Giv'at ha-Mivtar," *Israel Exploration Journal* 20 (1970).
[110] Zias and Sekeles, "The Crucified Man," 42.
[111] Ibid., 58.

die of asphyxiation, experiencing extreme difficulty breathing out and needing to raise themselves up to breathe in. This explanation is only a hypothesis, however, and not an accepted fact. Defenders of the hypothesis have used experimental data as evidence; these include the Austrian radiologist Hermann Moedder in a 1940s study. To prove the asphyxiation theory, Moedder suspended volunteer medical students by the wrists with their hands raised and spread about forty inches apart. The study indicated that within six minutes the volunteers began to suffer oxygen deprivation.[112]

Frederick Zugibe questioned Moedder's conclusions, saying, "His experiments merely confirmed that asphyxiation could occur if a person is suspended by the hands directly above their head within 40 inches from each other. Moreover, Jesus was suspended on the cross for several hours not 10 minutes. There is no doubt that if Jesus was suspended with his hands in the same manner, there would be difficulty breathing, but not so if the victim is suspended with his arms at an angle of between 65 to 70 degrees."[113] Zugibe pointed out that Moedder had failed to discover the physiological symptoms associated with varying the degrees of the victims' suspended arms. However, Zugibe better dictates his concern with the hypothesis by pointing out the severe events that the man in the Shroud had experienced even before being raised on the cross:

> Could a person in a state of traumatic and hypovolemic shock who had undergone severe anxiety to a point of hematidrosis [sweating blood], had been brutally scourged

---

[112] H. Moedder, "Die Todersursache Bei der Kreuzigung," *Stimmen der Zeit* (1949).
[113] Zugibe, *The Crucifixion of Jesus*, 99.

with a flagrum, suffered trigeminal neuralgia from the crowning with thorns, stumbled and fell for a half mile carrying a 50 pound cross part of the way, then nailed through the hands and feet with large spike-like nails and suspended on a cross be able to repeatedly push and pull themselves up against the spike-like nails in their swollen, exquisitely tender hands and feet in order to breathe over a period of several hours? I don't think so![114]

Instead, Zugibe explained the death of crucifixion by pointing at the detrimental and lethal effects of what had happened to this person preceding the nailing and suspension. He used an experiment of his own to disprove Moedder's results. Zugibe suspended twenty- to thirty-five-year-old volunteers for five to forty-five minutes, depending on when they wished to come down. Most were taken down due to cramping; not a single volunteer reported symptoms of oxygen deprivation. Examining the volunteers immediately after their descent, Zugibe recorded that the oxygen levels in their blood had either increased or remained constant. Due to the results of the experiment, Zugibe concluded that Christ more likely died of blood loss than of asphyxiation. Following the details of "The Way of the Cross," the researcher noted that the high blood loss would have caused traumatic and hypovolemic shock, meaning that the heart was unable to pump enough blood to the body.

As with nearly everything in science, even the outcome of experiments is rarely conclusive. Who is right in this dispute? It looks as if Zugibe's hypothesis is more likely, but a combination may be possible, too. Science never gives us final, definite answers, though. There is always room for discussion and improvements.

[114] Ibid., 95.

So we must come to the conclusion that science does not have the last word, not even in anatomical analysis, when it comes to the Shroud of Turin. Yet it should not contradict what faith tells us and may even confirm what we know based on faith. An openness to religious faith may add new elements and insights beyond the scope of the anatomical analysis done by science.

6

Textile Analysis

Being a cloth, and thus a textile, the Shroud of Turin lends itself to be studied by textile experts. Let's find out what they have to say about the material of the Shroud and about the story it may have to tell.

The Shroud of Turin — in Italian, *Sindone di Torino* — is a burial shroud made of high-quality linen woven in a three-over-one herringbone pattern, measuring 434 by 112 centimeters (14 feet, 3 inches by 3 feet, 8 inches) with a side strip of 7.6 centimeters (3 inches) sewn lengthwise on one of the long sides. As made apparent by the image, it covered a man who had suffered wounds very similar, or perhaps identical, to those inflicted upon Jesus of Nazareth during His Crucifixion.

What Is the Shroud Made Of?

Linen, the material of the Shroud, is made of hand-spun flax — a strong fiber, finer and more textured than cotton, with the linen thread coming from the stems of the flax plant. Unfortunately, the terminology used in the textile discussion is not very refined or consistent. Some make no distinction between flax and cotton, or between cotton and linen, even though coming from different plants. To make the situation even more confusing, flax is sometimes connected with a plant called *Linum usitatissimum* and other times is connected with a plant classified as *Gossypium herbaceum*, also called "levant cotton" or "cotton plant," which is a species of plant native to the semiarid regions of the Near East. Textile experts are not necessarily botanical experts. Besides, plant taxonomy is not the best kind of science, as the next chapter will affirm; it's still in a mainly descriptive stage.

Flax is grown in the region extending from the eastern Mediterranean to India, where it was most likely first domesticated and cultivated as well. Known to be one of the oldest fiber crops in the world, flax has been grown for at least five thousand years.[115] The best crops make the finest linens, such as the one exhibited by the Shroud of Turin. The thickness of the fibers from flax plants varies significantly, with an average of twelve to sixteen micrometers in diameter. The average thickness of the Shroud fibers is about thirteen micrometers, which makes for very fine fibers.

3D digital illustrator Ray Downing explains that linens are made by spinning the flax fibers either clockwise, forming a Z-shape, or counterclockwise, forming an S-shape, and weaving them in a herringbone twill (an intricate three-over-one pattern). Over the centuries, fibers have usually been spun counterclockwise, as the flax tends to form an S-shape naturally. But instead of following the trend, the fibers of the Shroud have been spun counterclockwise, forming a Z-shaped twist.[116]

---

[115] A. J. Wardey, *The Linen Trade: Ancient and Modern* (Abington, UK: Routledge, 1967), 752.

[116] Ray Downing, "The Fabric of the Shroud of Turin," Ray Downing, March 30, 2017, https://www.raydowning.com/blog/2017/2/23/the-fabric-of-the-shroud-of-turin.

According to textile analytics and the intricate three-over-one pattern in which it was woven, the linen of the Shroud is considered to be finely made, which parallels the linen's origins, revealed in the New Testament. The cloth is attributed to Joseph of Arimathea, the man who, according to all four Gospels, assumed responsibility for the burial of Jesus after His Crucifixion. The Gospel of St. Matthew describes him explicitly as a "rich man,"[117] who presumably had the wealth to purchase a "fine linen."

Mark narrates that, after being given permission by Pontius Pilate to take away the body of Jesus, Joseph immediately "bought a linen shroud, and taking him down, wrapped him in the linen shroud."[118] According to St. John's Gospel, Joseph and Nicodemus took the body and bound it in linen cloths with the spices that Nicodemus had bought.[119] In fact, all four Gospels mention that Jesus' followers wrapped his body with a linen cloth.[120]

St. John—known for being the most detailed in his descriptions—tells us in his Gospel, "Simon Peter ... went into the tomb; he saw the linen cloths lying, and the napkin, which had been on his head, not lying with the linen cloths [plural] but rolled up in a place by itself."[121] This episode makes it clear to us that we are dealing with not only a burial cloth (the Shroud), but also cloth bands and a face cloth—apparently all made of fine linen.

It has been mentioned by some that the linen came from India. It could have reached Palestine and been purchased through the extensive trade route between the Far East and the Middle

---

[117] Matt. 27:57.
[118] Mark 15:46.
[119] John 19:38–40.
[120] Matt. 27:59; Mark 15:46; Luke 23:53; John 19:40.
[121] John 20:6–7.

East, known as the Silk Road. Whether the Shroud came from India or had only been touched by people from India, we know there is some connection with India. Is it important to know? Not really, as long as we realize the Shroud carries many secrets and keeps surprising us. Unfortunately, however, the fine linen of the Shroud not only comes with welcome surprises but also with troublesome surprises—by being contaminated through touching hands and by being damaged through fire.

How Fire Damaged the Shroud

The Shroud as we know it today shows two clear sets of fire damage. Ultraviolet fluorescence has confirmed the two kinds of fire stains.[122] Damages caused during the fire of 1532 show a reddish fluorescence, indicating that the cloth smoldered in an encased environment of low oxygen. The other fire stains do not have the red fluorescence but do have a burnt rim around the edge, which indicates a more open fire.

The most obvious fire marks were caused during the fire of 1532, but a smaller, painted replica of the Shroud, located in the Saint Gommaire church in Lier, Belgium, indicates that the other fire must have preceded this date.[123] The replica dates to 1516 and depicts the image with only four of the burns we see on it today.[124]

---

[122] V.D. Miller et al., "Ultraviolet Fluorescence Photography of the Shroud of Turin," *Journal of Biological Photography* 49, no. 3 (July 1981): 71–85.

[123] Ian Wilson, *The Blood and the Shroud* (Tampa: The Free Press, 1998), 288.

[124] J.C. Iannone, *The Mystery of the Shroud of Turin: New Scientific Evidence* (Staten Island, NY: St. Paul's, 1998), 4.

Therefore, there must have been a previous fire that had damaged the Shroud, although to a lesser degree, before 1516.

The *Pray Codex*, dated to the early 1190s, also displays a shroud with four clear L-shaped holes. These holes must be the marks of the fire that had damaged the Shroud at some date prior to 1190.[125]

Nevertheless, the fire in Sainte-Chapelle, Chambéry, on December 4, 1532, inflicted the most significant damage on the Shroud. It had been kept in the chapel in a silver box that partially melted in the heat of the fire. Drops of silver damaged the folded corners of the cloth but, almost miraculously, did not affect the image of the body. The Poor Clares of Chambéry carefully and reverently patched the burned marks with material that textile analysis reveals to be dyed cotton fibers, as opposed to the original flax-fiber linen. In addition, they reinforced the ancient cloth by attaching the linen to new material that dates to Europe between 1532 and 1534.[126] This practice of affixing older cloth to newer was not unusual — the support cloth is known as the "Holland cloth," or "Dutch cloth."[127]

The Shroud underwent further repair in 1694 by Sebastian Valfrè, a member of the Oratory of St. Philip Neri,[128] as well as in 1868 by Princess Clotilde of the House of Savoy[129] Each time,

---

[125] Ibid., 154–155.

[126] Raymond N. Rogers, "Studies on the Radiocarbon Sample from the Shroud of Turin," *Thermochimica Acta* 425 (2005): 190, posted on Collegamento pro Sindone, http://www.sindone.info/ROGERS-3.PDF.

[127] Originally the name was applied to any fine, plain-woven linens imported from Europe, particularly from the Netherlands.

[128] John Beldon Scott, *Architecture for the Shroud: Relic and Ritual in Turin* (Chicago: University of Chicago Press, 2003), 26.

[129] Arthur Stapylton Barnes, *Holy Shroud of Turin* (WhiteFish, MT: Kessinger Publishing, 2010), 62.

those repairing the Shroud had the intention of improving its durability and appearance for public display and veneration. The holy cloth remained in the possession of the Savoys until the end of their rule in 1946. In 1983, it was donated to the Holy See, under whose ownership it now remains.

It was Gilbert Raes from the Ghent Institute of Textile Technology in Belgium who confirmed the difference in fabrics, between "old" linens and "new" materials within the Shroud.[130] Raes reported that the original linens were an ancient Near Eastern variety of *Gossypium herbaceum*, which grows typically in the Middle East. He based his report on the distance between reversals in the tape-shaped flax fibers (about eight per centimeter). This discovery made it extremely likely that the cloth had been made in the Middle East.

The Shroud has undergone restoration as recently as 2002 as well, when the Vatican allowed Mechthild Flury-Lemberg of Switzerland and her team of textile experts to unstitch the patches put in nearly five hundred years earlier by the Poor Clares. The team undid many of the old repairs, including removing the Holland cloth, which enabled the back of the Shroud to be photographed for the first time. The work of this team of experts also allowed for continued investigation into the mysterious fabric.

One of the mysteries of the Shroud of Turin is the presence of the so-called "side strip" — a strip of linen about 7.6 centimeters wide (3 inches) and 4.3 meters long (14 feet, 3 inches) with only a single seam affixing it to the left side of the Shroud (when looking at the image upright). A significant portion of

---

[130] Gilbert Raes, "Appendix B-Rapport d'Analise, La Santa Sindone," supplement to *Rivista Diocesana Torinese* (January 1976): 79–83.

the side cloth, however, appears to be missing: 14 centimeters (5.5 inches) from the bottom and 36 centimeters (14 inches) from the top left-hand corner.

What is the origin and purpose of this strip? Was it added later? If so, when? These questions have haunted those who study the Shroud. One thing seems to be evident: the side strip is made from the same piece of linen as the Shroud. They both have a twill herringbone weave, with the same textile irregularities. They also both showcase the same threading. The thread in the side seam imitates that of the Shroud in identical fiber thickness and weaving pattern, strongly suggesting that the two pieces were made of the same fabric.

This analysis raises the question of when the side strip was detached from or attached to the main cloth. Chemical analysis by Alan Adler and his team confirmed that the side strip predates the fabric of the 1534 repairs, further allowing for the likely possibility that the two pieces of cloth share the same date of origin.[131] Flury-Lemberg then discovered "a peculiar stitching pattern in the seam of one long side of the Shroud, where a three-inch-wide strip of the same original fabric was sewn onto a larger segment."[132]

Only on one other occasion in her forty-year career had the textile expert run into this "essentially identical" type of stitching. At the 2000 Turin Symposium, Flury-Lemberg reported that the matching sample had been discovered in tombs just outside Masada, Israel. This geographical region contains the ruins of

---

[131] John Heller and Alan Adler: "A Chemical Investigation of the Shroud of Turin," *Canadian Society of Forensic Science Journal* 14 (1981): 81–103.

[132] Mechthild Flury-Lemberg, "Tapestries," in *Textile Conservation and Research* (Bern: Abegg-Stiftung, 1988).

a Jewish fortress sacked by the Romans at the end of the First Jewish-Roman War, between AD 66 and AD 73. The cloth itself, exhibiting the same professional-level weaving as the Shroud, dated to the first century, between 40 BC and AD 73—right around the same time as the death and burial of Jesus.[133] The similarities between this sample and the Shroud are astounding. The expert further notes that "this kind of stitch has never been found on cloths from Medieval Europe."[134]

We speculate that the side strip was taken from the main cloth in order to bind it around the body. This explains why the Gospel speaks of cloths, in the plural, found lying in the tomb after the Resurrection. Soon after, someone likely sewed the side strip back onto the main cloth, so that the two pieces would stay together. Tradition tells us it was our Lady who did so before her nephew Thaddeus brought the holy cloths to Edessa. Perhaps later, the side strip was used to preserve the main cloth from potential damages in handling or displaying the Shroud.

But this still leaves us with the question of why there are pieces missing at both ends of the cloth's strip. Adler mentions the possibility that certain dignitaries were given pieces of the Shroud as gifts throughout history.[135] If such a practice had been caried out, naturally pieces would have been taken from the ends in order to preserve the image of the Shroud.

---

[133] Ian Wilson, *The Shroud: The 2000-Year-Old Mystery Solved* (London: Bantam Press, 2010), 74.

[134] Flury-Lemberg, "Tapestries."

[135] Alan D. Adler, "Concerning the Side Strip on the Shroud of Turin" (1997), Shroud of Turin website, https://www.shroud.com/adler2.htm.

How Old Is the Textile?

From what we have seen so far, given the fact that the Shroud of Turin has two kinds of burn marks, the cloth must date to at least 1516, the time when a copy of the Shroud detailed marks of the first fire. Another time indication comes from the *Pray Codex*, which is dated to the 1190s. But even that time frame is far from the Crucifixion and burial of Jesus. So, the question remains: Could the Shroud be from the time of Jesus, or is it a textile that was woven more than a millennium later?

There are several indications that the Shroud does date back to the time of Jesus' Crucifixion. We mentioned already that the weaving pattern of the Shroud and the stitching of the side seam are characteristic of Jewish burial practices that date back to first-century Israel. Beyond the evidence of the Masada cloth, we can observe the striking similarities with the linen wrappings of the Dead Sea scrolls.

While this might not strike modern audiences as odd, it is worth pointing out that there are no animal hairs on the Shroud. This is quite telling because the Laws of Moses prescribe that wool, being the product of sheep hair, and linen must not be mixed.[136] The absence of animal hair further authenticates the Shroud's potential use by a Jew and potential use by the people who buried Jesus.

Another peculiar feature of the Shroud is its size. It is approximately 434 centimeters by 112 centimeters (14 feet, 4 inches by 3 feet, 8 inches), depending on conditions of humidity and on which parts are included.[137] This appears to be an odd size but not when converted to the Assyrian standard unit of cubits,

[136] Deut. 22:11.
[137] Zugibe, *The Crucifixion of Jesus*, 174.

which was presumably the common unit of lineal measurement in Jesus' day.[138] The Assyrian sizing of the Shroud exactly aligns with the dimensions dictated by Jewish burial practices.[139]

Chemical tests provide more confirmation for the age of the Shroud—one of which was developed by chemist Raymond Rogers from Los Alamos National Laboratory. Rogers discovered the presence of vanillin, a product of a chemical compound found in flax. As the compound breaks down over time, vanillin is released, but as more time passes, the vanillin levels decline. According to Rogers's studies, it would take more than 1,300 years for the fibers in the Shroud to lose 95 percent of their vanillin at a consistent 77 degrees Fahrenheit (25 degrees Celsius). At about 73 degrees Fahrenheit (23 degrees Celsius), it would take about 1,800 years, and at 68 degrees Fahrenheit (20 degrees Celsius), it would take more than 3,000 years. Both the Shroud and the linen wrappings of the Dead Sea Scrolls contain no vanillin. With the scrolls dating between 300 BC and AD 300, we can estimate the ancient nature of the Shroud in comparison. While this method doesn't give an exact date to the Shroud, it can help us approximate it. This finding led Rogers to conclude: "Because the shroud and other very old linens do not give the vanillin test, the cloth must be quite old."[140] In other words, the Shroud of Turin could very well date back to our Lord's Crucifixion.

In addition, Professor Giulio Fanti, professor at the University of Padua's Engineering Faculty, developed other tests for dating

---

[138] Mark Antonacci, *The Resurrection of the Shroud* (New York: M. Evans, 2000), 1.

[139] Ian Dickinson, "The Shroud and the Cubit Measure," *British Society for the Turin Shroud Newsletter*, no. 24, January 1990, 8–11.

[140] Rogers, "Studies on the Radiocarbon Sample," 191.

ancient materials such as the Shroud of Turin—including the so-called compressibility and breaking-strength tests. With these tests, Fanti could determine that the origin of the Shroud occurred around AD 400, plus or minus four hundred years (with a 95 percent confidence level)—which amounts to between AD 1 and 800.[141] Fanti's tests were corroborated by Universities of Padua, Bologna, Modena, Udine, Parma, and London. This would, again (although roughly), date the Shroud to a time commensurate with the life and Crucifixion of Jesus.

Let's summarize our findings. The hand-made linen was of professional quality, and its sewing technique places it in Israel in the first century AD. If the Shroud of Turin did travel the route we described previously, we may confidently assume it's not only a Shroud of Israel or Jerusalem but also the Shroud of Jesus.

So we must come to the conclusion that science does not have the last word, not even in textile analysis, when it comes to the Shroud of Turin. Once again, reason will not contradict faith, and faith might even add to our knowledge of things beyond science's scope.

---

[141] Angela Ambrogetti, "The Shroud, the Real Problem Is the Image," July 5, 2019, posted on the Shroud of Turin website, https://www.shroud.com/pdfs/ACIstampa3.pdf.

7

Pollen Analysis

Pollen is a powdery substance that contains pollen grains. The grains have a hard coat that protects them as they move from the "male" parts of flowering plants to their "female" parts. Pollen grains themselves are highly diverse in appearance, depending on the kind of plant from which they originate. The superficial characteristics, such as shape, size, and surface patterns, can be studied by using light microscopy or scanning electron microscopy.

Grains of pollen, especially from wind-pollinated plants and trees, are produced and disseminated every year in huge quantities. The grains have a woody wall that can survive for thousands of years. Since the shape of the wall is typical for various species of plants, different areas with different vegetations produce different kinds of pollen grains.

What Pollen Grains Tell Us about the Shroud

Generally speaking, pollen analysis compares older pollen samples with younger ones—ones whose parent plants and environments are known.[142] Of course, this assumes that pollen grains

[142] J. T. Overpeck et al., "Quantitative Interpretation of Fossil Pollen Spectra: Dissimilarity Coefficients and the Method of Modern Analogs," *Quaternary Research* 23 (1985): 87-108.

haven't changed shape through history, but that is usually a fair assumption.

In 1973, some clerics in Turin asked Max Frei-Sulzer, a well-known forensic scientist from Switzerland, to examine the Shroud with a microscope and to apply to it a method he had developed to unravel crimes. Frei was familiar with botany and had written a thesis on the subject. With this background knowledge, he took sticky tape samples from the Shroud of Turin, drawing dust and pollen from the surface of the linen for analysis.

When he studied the particles under a microscope, he found pollen grains from fifty-eight species of plants—with seventeen being indigenous to Europe (including Lirey and Chambéry), but the majority representing plants indigenous to the area of the Dead Sea and Turkey. These species included *Hyoscyamus aureus*, *Artemisia herba-alba*, and *Onosma syriacum*.[143] Frei also detected pollen grains of *Zygophyllum dumosum*—a species unique to Israel.

Frei's results were confirmed in a study by Avinoam Danin, a prominent Israeli botanist and professor at Hebrew University in Jerusalem.[144] Danin discovered twenty-eight species of pollen and labeled many of them unique to Jerusalem. In his 2010 publication, the botanist wrote, "March-April is the time of year when the whole assemblage of some 10 of the plants identified on the Shroud is in bloom," indicating that the cloths would have been used most likely in the spring months—the time of year when the Church commemorates the Passion, death, and Resurrection of Christ.

[143] Max Frei-Sulzer, "Nine Years of Palynological Studies on the Shroud," *Shroud Spectrum International* 3 (1982): 2–7.

[144] Avinoam Danin, *Botany of the Shroud of Turin: The Story of Floral Images on the Shroud of Turin* (Jerusalem: Danin Publishing, 2010).

There is one problem with these conclusions, though. It is hard to tell whether the pollens Frei had picked up with his sticky tape were from the beginning period of the Shroud or from pollens later acquired during the transportation and the expositions of the cloth.

The Pitfalls of Pollen Analysis

There is another, more serious problem with pollen analysis. It's not quite possible to determine all pollen grains to the level of a *species*, but at best to a wider category, such as a *genus*, or an even wider taxon, which increases the number of species included. So pollen grains may be unique to a certain genus only—for example, *Zygophyllum*—but not to a certain species—such as *Zygophyllum dumosum*. The subgenus level of a taxon is not near enough to the species level that is often needed to determine the area of origin for each plant.

Is this detrimental for our use of pollen analysis? Not quite. First, the species concept in botany is still rather murky. It is based more on morphology than on genetics. Many well-accepted plant species can interbreed, at least potentially, which is contrary to the accepted biological-species concept used for the rest of the living world. The reason might be that plants don't always reject pollen grains coming from similar species that are not their own.

Another reason might be that botanists are simply splitting species too much. The common dandelion plant, for instance, is considered by some botanists to consist of more than a hundred species, but others regard it as a single one. In general, botanists still use the "type" definition of a species, which is often a specimen stored in an herbarium for further reference. Based on this definition, it is similarity between plants that is used to designate their presumed species status—which is a rather imprecise way of making scientific decisions.

Are there better ways to determine the origin of pollen grains and their species? There is a way if we switch from determination by light microscopy to determination by scanning electron microscopy, for the latter reveals many more surface details; but this method has not yet been done consistently with Shroud samples. Switching to the new method may not end up adding much more precision and certainty after all, due to the difficulty in determining a plant's area of origin, despite more visible surface details. As a matter of fact, even with help coming from DNA research, the subgenus level that has been reached is not near enough to the species level that is needed to determine the area of origin for each plant and its pollen grains.

What new forms of DNA research have done for us, though, is show the diversity of pollen grains found on the Shroud over a long period of time. This research tells us we cannot assume that all pollen grains found on the Shroud have come from the Shroud's land of origin. Gianni Barcaccia, a specialist in genetics and genomics, used the National Center for Biotechnology Information database of DNA sequences to compare pollen grains on the basis of chloroplast DNA (cpDNA). He noticed that "among the NCBI sequences most similar to those obtained from the Shroud, one belongs to a spruce tree sampled in the Swiss Alps.... This discovery is in accord with the transport of the Shroud through the French-Italian Alps in 1578 when the relic was moved from Chambéry to Turin."[145]

---

[145] Gianni Barcaccia et al., "Uncovering the sources of DNA found on the Turin Shroud," *Nature, Scientific Reports* 5, no. 14484 (2015): 6.

Barcaccia found even more diversity of pollen evidence. As he put it, "Several plant taxa native to the Mediterranean area were identified as well as species with a primary center of origin in Asia, the Middle East or the Americas but introduced in a historical interval later than the Medieval period."[146] This discovery, that pollen grains on the Shroud came from all over the world, should not surprise us. Plants from Asia may have been introduced into the Near East after the travels of Marco Polo, and plants from the Americas came to the Mediterranean after Columbus's discovery of the continent. They could easily have ended up on the Shroud during its transportation and during the times it was displayed.

Many conclude from this explanation that the science of pollen analysis cannot prove much about the origin of the Shroud of Turin. But even if it could, we must take such scientific "proof" with a grain of salt. The truth of the matter is, again, that science cannot prove anything with absolute certainty—at best it can confirm its conclusions to a higher degree. Therefore, pollen analysis can make it only more likely or less likely, for instance, that the Shroud came from Jerusalem. But it can never *prove* that it did or did not. This is not because pollen analysis is inadequate but because science and the scientific enterprise as such are inherently limited. As we discussed earlier, science cannot prove anything with absolute certainty.

If science cannot prove, however, perhaps it can *disprove*. Some have objected, for instance, that Frei never found pollen grains of the olive tree (*Olea europaea*), which are not difficult to identify and are very widespread in the Middle East. Isn't this a form of falsification that nullifies Frei's data? Doesn't this

[146] Ibid., 1.

disprove the likelihood of the Shroud's having originated in Jerusalem?

Not really. The lack of olive pollen grains on the Shroud does not automatically invalidate Frei's findings. As we found out earlier, absence of evidence—lack of olive pollen grains—does not amount to evidence of absence—certain evidence that the Shroud is a fake. At best, it may only make Frei's findings less convincing. The fact that we have never found life without DNA or RNA, which is absence of evidence, doesn't mean that there is no life without DNA or RNA, which would be evidence of absence. The question is always whether we *could* have detected some evidence if it exists.

Why can this finding not even disprove Frei's data? It is always possible to undermine counterevidence and then discard it; therefore, falsification is never detrimental in science—it merely teaches us something more. There are always ways to argue against falsifying evidence. One could, for instance, counter that the olive tree is mainly pollinated by insects rather than by the wind. To this claim, Ian Wilson and Barrie Schwortz responded, "It would have required an insect to have been on an olive tree just before landing on the Shroud during the burial or during one of its open-air expositions—a very rare chance indeed."[147]

In other words, there is always the benefit of the doubt, even in science. There is always the possibility to question the evidence brought in against a certain hypothesis. Perhaps the evidence that was brought in is based on dubious assumptions or on misinterpreted data. If that's the case, then the "facts" we thought we had cannot be facts. Perhaps the season wasn't right for pollination

---

[147] Ian Wilson and Barrie Schwortz, *The Turin Shroud: The Illustrated Evidence* (London: Michael O'Mara Books, 2000), 88–90.

when the Shroud was used for burial, or the sample of pollen grains taken from the Shroud was too small, or the sample was taken from the wrong area of the cloth, or the outcome was caused by any other explanation we hadn't thought of. When research seems to say no to a hypothesis, we don't really know what exactly it is that research says no to.

This means there is no proof, based on pollen analysis, that the Shroud of Turin is the Shroud of Jesus, nor is there proof that the Shroud of Turin is *not* the Shroud of Jesus—at least not in the sense of "proof" that comes with complete certainty. Well, that wasn't to be expected anyway—only mathematics can really prove its conclusions once we accept its axioms. Science can never prove or disprove anything beyond reasonable doubt. It can only lend more, or at times less, credibility to its scientific claims. Pollen analysis has given us more credibility but certainly not final credibility. No part of science can.

The best that pollen analysis can tell us, with a good level of confidence, is that the Shroud displayed in Turin is a shroud that came from Judea but then went through many journeys and was in contact with many people and surroundings.

The Crown of Thorns

The crown, or cap, of thorns seems to be unique to the Crucifixion of Jesus, so we found out. The crown is not mentioned, however, by any sources other than the Bible until the fifth century.[148] Yet the Shroud clearly shows wounds that were caused

---

[148] Charles Wall, *Relics from the Crucifixion: Where They Went and How They Got There* (Manchester, NH: Sophia Institute Press, 2016), 95.

by a crown of thorns—which is another confirmation of the Shroud's authenticity as the burial cloth of Jesus.

Is it possible to discover which thorns were used in the crown? Frederick Zugibe, the chief medical examiner of Rockland County, New York, and professor of pathology at Columbia University, mentions that "the tortuous flows on the forehead and the significant amount of blood on the head region had to have been the result of penetration of the skin by sharp thorns from plants like those of *Ziziphus spina* or *Ziziphus paliuris*, both of the Buckthorn family (*Rhamnaceae*)."[149] Using forensic analysis, he also notes that "*Ziziphus spina christi* (Syrian Christ thorn) or *Ziziphus paliuris christi* (Christ's thorn) would cause puncture-type wounds with significant bleeding when struck with the reed ... accounting for the blood flows and accumulations of blood in the head region of the Shroud."[150] It should be noted, too, that both species of thorns can also be plaited into a cap of thorns, adding a greater surface area of thorns per unit of skin contact.

However, forensic evidence is not enough to decide this issue. We need to know whether these plants existed at the time of Jesus in the area of Jerusalem. Michael Evanari, professor of botany at the University of Jerusalem, reported to Zugibe that *Ziziphus spina* is found at the southern border of Israel and to some extent in Samaria, but not in Jerusalem or its surroundings today.[151] As a result, he considered it improbable that it grew in Jerusalem during Jesus' time. But he also added, wisely, that no one can be certain. This conclusion might make another species

---

[149] Zugibe, *The Crucifixion of Jesus*, 28.

[150] Zugibe, *Forensic and Clinical Knowledge*.

[151] M. Evanari, personal communication, October 10, 1964 (mentioned in Zugibe, ibid.).

a more likely candidate for the crown of thorns, since this species "would cause puncture-type wounds with significant bleeding when struck with the reed."[152]

Another candidate for the crown of thorns might be the thorny acacia (*Acacia nilotica*), which can be found in abundance in and around Jerusalem. Remarkably, a crown of thorns made from this plant was unearthed by archaeologist Robin Hewitt in a sarcophagus dated 1189.[153] That doesn't prove much, of course, but it is noteworthy.

Again, no decision can be made on this information alone. Perhaps pollen analysis can help us further. The botanist Danin has suggested that the thorns of the tumbleweed *Gundelia tournefortii*, a member of the thistle family, were used for the crown or cap.[154] One of his reasons for believing so is that large amounts of the plant's pollen were found on the Shroud of Turin.

That's where controversy comes in again. For instance, Vaughn Bryant from the Palynology Laboratory at Texas A&M University claims that this research is not definitive because it was based only on light microscopy, rather than scanning electron microscopy, the latter of which would reveal many more surface details.[155] Furthermore, *Gundelia tournefortii* is a prickly plant, not a thorny plant. It is also a common tumbleweed in the region, which might explain why many pollens of the plant were found on the Shroud

---

[152] Zugibe, *Forensic and Clinical Knowledge.*

[153] Ibid., 32.

[154] Reported by William K. Stevens, "Tests Trace Turin Shroud to Jerusalem before A.D. 700," *New York Times*, August 3, 1999, https://www.nytimes.com/1999/08/03/world/tests-trace-turin-shroud-to-jerusalem-before-ad-700.html.

[155] Vaughn Bryant, "Does Pollen Prove the Shroud Authentic?," *Biblical Archaeology Review* 26, no. 6 (2000).

of Turin anyway. But it is unlikely to have caused the profuse head wounds exhibited by the image. Apparently, we end up again with an undecided issue as far as science is concerned. Perhaps other scientific tools might help us further.

So, once again, we must come to the conclusion that science does not have the last word, not even in pollen analysis, when it comes to the Shroud of Turin. We must also remember reason's inherent compatibility with faith as we continue our scientific study.

8

Carbon Analysis

If you want to know the date of an object, such as the Shroud, science recommends carbon dating. Carbon dating has the aura of scientific precision when historical records fail. Understandably, as more and more data became available about the Shroud of Turin, the interest in its dating reached a climax, and the Vatican decided to allow carbon testing on a small piece of the cloth.

Two experts, Franco Testore, professor of textile technology at the Turin Polytechnic, and Gabriel Vial, curator of the Ancient Textile Museum in Lyon, France, determined the area to sample, although chemist Raymond Rogers reveals that "the operation was done in secrecy, and no chemical investigations were made at the time to test the sample."[156] A small corner of the Shroud was cut for radiocarbon dating and sent for analysis to three laboratories: in Oxford, Zurich, and Tucson, Arizona. In 1988, these three radiocarbon laboratories united in the following conclusion: "The age of the shroud is obtained as AD 1260–1390, with at least 95% confidence."[157]

[156] Rogers, "Studies on the Radiocarbon Sample," 189.
[157] P. E. Damon et al., "Radiocarbon Dating of the Shroud of Turin," *Nature* 337 (1989): 611–615, posted on the Shroud of Turin website, https://www.shroud.com/nature.htm.

These results were not what many people had expected. It was earth-shattering news that has been heavily debated ever since—and rightly so, for several reasons.

What Is Carbon Dating?

Carbon dating is more precisely called radiocarbon dating. Every chemical element has its own kind of nucleus, made up of a specific number of protons—the element's atomic number—together with some number of neutrons, which differs and affects the atomic mass of various isotopes. An atom of the element carbon, for instance, has exactly six protons in its nucleus. One isotope of carbon also has six neutrons, making for an atomic mass of twelve. Therefore, it is called "carbon 12." Another carbon isotope has eight neutrons, which makes for "carbon 14."

How can carbon help us to date things? The secret can be found in the existence of isotopes. Isotopes of a particular element differ in the number of neutrons in their nuclei. Some isotopes are inherently unstable or radioactive. That is, at some point, an atom of such an isotope will undergo radioactive decay and spontaneously transform into a different atom or atoms. The decay follows a particular pattern. The number of radioactive isotopes will be reduced in half after a certain time interval, specific for each radioactive isotope. With the passing of the next interval (of the same amount of time), it will be reduced by half again: from 50 percent to 25 percent to 12.5 percent, and so on. This time interval is called an isotope's half-life.

The term "radiocarbon" is commonly used to refer to ^{14}C, an isotope of carbon (C) that is radioactive with a half-life of about 5,730 years plus or minus 40 years—which means that the amount of radioactive carbon is cut in half every 5,730 years;

so after 11,460 years, only a quarter is left; after 17,190 years, only an eighth; and so on. Samples 50,000 or 60,000 years old have so little carbon 14 left that accurate radiocarbon dating is no longer possible.

When first developing radiocarbon dating in the late 1940s, Willard Libby studied the natural and constant production of radiocarbon in Earth's atmosphere, forming when cosmic rays combine with atmospheric nitrogen. The ^{14}C then joins with oxygen to make radioactive carbon dioxide ($^{14}CO_2$), which, in turn, is taken in by plants during photosynthesis and by animals when they eat plants.

As soon as a plant or animal dies, it stops assimilating carbon from its environment, and the amount of ^{14}C starts to decline. Hence, after about 5,730 years, half of its ^{14}C will have decayed. The process of measuring this radioactive decay can be applied to plants or animals, and because the Shroud is composed of linens from flax plants, the technique was used to estimate the date that the plant (from which the cloth was made) died.

Is the result of a radiocarbon test etched in stone? No, it is not. The outcome of each test varies, but it does follow what is called a normal distribution of measurements. This means that data points can end up on either side of the measured value, which explains the practice to report the calculated dates with a margin of error of at least one standard deviation (SD). One SD gives a 68 percent chance that the "real" value lies within the presented range, but because a 68 percent confidence level is not very high, most resort to ranges of two SD, raising the confidence level to a 95 percent chance. For instance, a laboratory ^{14}C measurement with a 68 percent confidence interval of 900 plus or minus 25 ^{14}C BP—which means the measurement of 900 years *before present* (BP) with a standard deviation of 25 years—covers a range between 875 and 925 years before present. To obtain a 95 percent confidence interval, this range should be doubled to twice the standard deviation—that is, to plus or minus 50, which leads to a range of 850–950 plus or minus 50 ^{14}C BP. It is a "certainty" of probabilities, however—nothing more.

Carbon-Dating the Shroud

How was the Shroud tested with carbon dating? The 1988 sampling operation was described by Paul Damon, a geoscientist of the University of Arizona who was a member of the testing team himself: "The shroud was separated from the backing cloth along its bottom left-hand edge and a strip (10 mm [by] 70 mm) was cut from just above the place where a sample was previously removed in 1973 for examination. The strip came from a single site on the main body of the shroud away from any patches or charred areas."[158]

Based on sound scientific standards, protocols had been set up ahead of time to guide the investigation of the Shroud and guarantee its validity. These protocols had been coordinated by the physicist Harry Gove at the spectrometry department of the University of Rochester and were accepted by the Vatican. This is what both parties had agreed upon: (1) samples were to be taken from multiple areas; (2) seven labs would participate; (3) the examinations would be simultaneous; (4) comparisons with known cloths would be blind; (5) no exchange of information would be allowed during the testing.[159]

---

[158] Damon et al., "Radiocarbon Dating."
[159] Harry Gove, *Relic, Icon or Hoax: Carbon Dating the Turin Shroud* (Bristol and Philadelphia: Institute of Physics Publishing, 1996), 83.

Contrary to the agreement, all these protocols were soon abandoned for several reasons. For instance, protocol 1 was not followed in order to protect the cloth and better preserve it. Other changes were advised by scientists such as Carlos Chagas, president of the Pontifical Academy of Science. The Vatican was given little choice but to accept the changes due to the political momentum of the issue.

Samples were given to a selection of laboratories, but the agreed-upon protocols were essentially abandoned. The seven laboratories as planned were eventually reduced to three: the laboratories of the University of Arizona, the University of Oxford, and the Polytechnic of Zurich. The main reason for the cutback, even in this decision, was to limit the number of samples taken from the Shroud.

Each lab received three control samples: a fragment of cloth from an Egyptian burial, which had been carbon-dated to AD 1100; a piece of mummy bandage, carbon-dated to AD 200; and a scrap of cloak having belonged to Louis IX of France, verifiably woven between 1240 and 1270.[160] The most disturbing issue was that the single sample taken from the Shroud could not have been taken from a less reliable place—a strip on the side. The sides would have been the portions of the holy cloth to be held and touched most during expositions and travel, which would easily skew tests such as carbon dating. This was quite inappropriate from a scientific point of view.

The three labs reported their results to the British Museum, where Michael Tite had been assigned to oversee the entire process and to communicate the official results to the Diocese of Turin and the Holy See. On October 13, 1988, Cardinal Ballestrero

---

[160] Ibid., 259, 270.

announced that radiocarbon testing had dated the Shroud to AD 1260–1390, with a 95 percent confidence level. The results were published in the prestigious scientific journal *Nature*[161] and made for earth-shattering news, as I mentioned earlier. This was all the evidence that Shroud skeptics needed to declare the cloth a fake.

The story took an unexpected turn, however. The published results of the ^{14}C tests did not cover all the data available because the British Museum, which oversaw the ^{14}C testing labs, had failed to provide complete data in the first place. For almost thirty years, Shroud scientists would be accusing the museum of keeping the raw data hidden under a "shroud" of secrecy, until the French researcher Tristan Casabianca filed a freedom-of-information request. Finally, in 2017, the museum complied with Casabianca's request and released the raw data.

Casabianca's team analyzed the data and concluded, "A statistical analysis of the *Nature* article and the raw data strongly suggest that homogeneity is lacking in the data and that the procedure should be reconsidered," effectively denouncing the results of the infamous radiocarbon testing.[162] The team found, for instance, numerous dates that fell outside the range published in *Nature*. Due to the questionable data, the 95 percent confidence level reported by the 1988 study came under scrutiny.

Casabianca's team admits that their statistical results "do not imply that the medieval hypothesis of the age of the tested sample should be ruled out," but they do discourage the quickness in accepting the hypothesis as true or even likely.[163]

---

[161] M. S. Tite, "Turin Shroud," *Nature* 332 (1988): 482.

[162] T. Casabianca et al., "Radiocarbon Dating of the Turin Shroud: New Evidence from Raw Data," *Archaeometry* (2019).

[163] Casabianca et al., 7.

Since evidence from other sources—such as historical analysis, computer analysis, anatomical analysis, textile analysis, and pollen analysis—seemed to indicate a date much older than 1260 for the Shroud of Turin, several scientists searched for other dating methods, apart from radiocarbon dating. Professor Fanti led a team of scientists from multiple Italian universities through three new tests of Shroud samples, reporting:

> The research includes three new tests, two chemical ones and one mechanical one. The first two were carried out with an FT-IR system, one using infra-red light and the other using Raman spectroscopy. The third was a multi-parametric mechanical test based on five different mechanical parameters linked to the voltage of the wire. The machine used to examine the Shroud's fibers and test traction allowed researchers to examine tiny fibers alongside about twenty samples of cloth dated between 3000 BC and 2000 AD.[164]

And this is how the team of scientists summarized their results:

> Final results show that the Shroud fibers examined produced the following dates, all of which are 95% certain and centuries away from the medieval dating obtained with Carbon-14 testing in 1988: the dates given to the Shroud after FT-IR testing, [are] 300 BC ±400, 200 BC ±500 after Raman testing and 400 AD ±400 after

---

[164] Giulio Fanti et al., "Non-Destructive Dating of Ancient Flax Textiles by Means of Vibrational Spectroscopy," *Vibrational Spectroscopy* 67 (2013): 61–70.

multi-parametric mechanical testing. The average of all three dates is 33 BC ±250 years.[165]

Fanti and his team found the average date of their discoveries to circle around AD 33 — the time consistently associated with the death of Jesus. The results of the study directly contradicted the 1988 results ascribing medieval origins to the Shroud. One might object that the ranges for each claim were too wide, but without drawing data from more samples, this outcome is to be expected. The scientists used only eight sample cloths for the FT-IR test, eleven for Raman, and twelve for the mechanical test. The scientists noted that "future calibrations based on a greater number of samples and coupled with ad-hoc cleaning procedures could significantly improve its accuracy, though it is not easy to find ancient samples adequate for the test."[166]

These alternative tests are not to discredit radiocarbon dating as a useful scientific tool. In the future, performing a second test with the Shroud may prove highly beneficial. Though the results of the 1988 test tell us that the cloth is a mere seven hundred years old, the findings are subject to change, as all scientific hypotheses are. Being aware of the pitfalls of radiocarbon dating, we just need to wait for the release of new samples from the Shroud before we attempt it again.

For many scientists, the results of carbon dating — supposedly given "in the name of science" and "with the authority of science" — were considered the final blow to believers in the authenticity of the Shroud. It remains the right and the duty of religious faith, however, to question what science claims to be

---

[165] Ibid.
[166] Ibid.

"the final truth." In other words, we need to discover the weak points in the scientific discussion of carbon analysis.

The Traps of Carbon Dating

It may not come easy for some scientists to criticize a favorite scientific tool. Carbon dating is standard nowadays, but the method is by no means infallible. It is based on various assumptions and is prone to errors in the testing procedure. In other words, so much can go wrong with this procedure that we should never put complete confidence in its outcome. There is always the benefit of the doubt. Carbon dating is merely a methodology. Its scientists are bright enough to master it but not always fair enough to criticize it.

How can there be such a wide difference between what science claims as the age of the Shroud—dating back to around 1300—and what many believers claim as the age of the Shroud —dating back to the first century AD? That's a difference of some thirteen centuries! Is there a way to explain such a large gap?

Some critics of carbon dating point to the lack of statistical assurance of the tests' results due to the normal distribution of errors. Outliers, false positives, and false negatives can be part of estimations such as these, and they have the possibility of skewing the results significantly, or even leading scientists down entirely wrong paths. Outliers represent data points that differ significantly from the general range of data, representing the extremes and throwing off averages. False positives show that something is present when, in fact, it is not, and false negatives show that something is not present when, in fact, it is. Each of these cases requires further statistical analysis to reduce the possibility of error. With all this said, and while these occurrences are not uncommon, it is unlikely that any of these factors can account for the huge difference between the two competing claims.

Other critics have questioned how accurate the measurements of carbon dating can be. Originally, radiocarbon was measured by using beta-counting devices, which counted the amount of beta radiation emitted by decaying ^{14}C atoms in a sample during the measurement. More recently, however, accelerator mass spectrometry has become a more reliable method of measurement, as it counts all the ^{14}C atoms in the sample. It is more reliable because it does not count just the few that happen to decay during the measurement. Another solution might be to increase the testing time, but any improvement made would not account for the difference in dating between 1200 and 30.

Critics remain inventive. They also have pointed out the atmospheric difference in the ratio of normal carbon (^{12}C) to radiocarbon (^{14}C) throughout history, claiming that it affects the accuracy of radiocarbon dating estimations. Because carbon and radiocarbon have not yet reached a state of equilibrium, results may be skewed. Considering earth's atmosphere post Industrial Revolution, more ^{14}C and more CO_2 exists in the air now than it did thousands of years ago. The difference in CO_2 is an estimated 40 percent increase—significant enough to throw off estimations. Furthermore, the ratio of carbon to radiocarbon fluctuates over short periods as well. Therefore, considering constants in an atmosphere that is so clearly fluctuating appears unreliable. However, it remains undetermined whether this observation, too, can explain the gap between the radiocarbon dating results and the date dictated by Christians.

There are many other possible sources of error as well. One of them is "operator contamination" of the data, which happens when people who handle the sample leave their own traces behind. Think of using a thermometer, which has its own temperature, to

measure the temperature of a sample. Of course, this kind of contamination must be avoided as much as possible by using extremely
strict protocols. Were those precautions taken during the testing?
They probably were. That takes the sting out of this objection.

A more serious critique comes from those who blame impurities in the sample for the dating results. It is to be expected that
samples of the Shroud may contain various kinds of impurities,
such as dyes that were added in the past, dirty hands that handled
and touched the cloth during its history, bacterial contamination,
and so on. Of course, the chance of contaminating impurities
can and must be reduced by applying "cleansing" or "purifying"
treatments to the sample. Different laboratories use different
methods to do so, however, and this introduces another degree of
variability. The purifying treatment may have its own unintended
effect on the sample. But again, is that enough to explain the
carbon-dating results? Probably not.

Is there a better argument to defend that the Shroud is some
twenty centuries old? I would say there is. The most powerful argument against the carbon-dating results is that the sample that was
taken from the Shroud and used for testing was not representative
of the whole. Using a single sample, on the assumption that it was
representative of the whole cloth, goes blatantly against standard
procedures, not to mention the protocols established before the
study. So the question is: What was "wrong" with that sample?
How did it misrepresent?

Well, there are several reasons this sample is of dubious origin.
First of all, the 1988 sample, cut in three, came from a single strip
from a single location on the Shroud—a serious methodological
mistake.

Second, we know from drawings made between 1690 and 1842
that the corner that was used for the carbon dating came from

the strip that used to be held suspended by a row of five bishops evenly spaced at each time the Shroud was on display. Frequent handling of the Shroud in this way increased the likelihood of contamination by bacteria and bacterial residue. Leftovers of bacteria and the products of bacterial metabolism carry their own ^{14}C that could very well move the radiocarbon date closer to 1300 and away from AD 30.

Third, the strip from which the samples were taken included repairs done to the Shroud after the fire of Chambéry in 1532. It was Rogers who discovered that the samples tested in the 1988 study had been taken from material that had been attached at a later date in order to repair pieces that had been worn down over centuries of veneration. He also found out that the testing sample had been dyed in the fourteenth century, with a dye that was not available in Europe until 1291.[167] So, one could certainly expect a carbon-dating result dated to the fourteenth century because all three labs took fibers from the same dyed strip.

Are these objections definitive for the debate about the age of the Shroud? To be fair, it must be stated that science cannot always provide us with the hard-core facts it is searching for. What we call "proven" scientific knowledge is proven only until a new set of empirical data "disproves" what was previously held. In science, whatever is true today may not be true tomorrow. Science is always a work in progress. Francis Crick, one of the two scientists who discovered DNA, couldn't have said it better: "A theory that fits all the facts is bound to be wrong, as some of the facts will be wrong."[168]

---

[167] B. Hochberg, *Handspinner's Handbook* (Norwalk, CT: Windham Center, 1980), 1–4.

[168] Francis Crick, *What Mad Pursuit: A Personal View of Scientific Discovery* (New York: Basics Books, 1990), 60.

Perhaps Crick should have expressed this more accurately: facts cannot be wrong, but they may turn out *not* to be facts. The widely accepted "fact" that the Shroud was not more than a thousand years old may have turned out not to be fact but fiction. The truth of the matter is that errors in procedure can also lead to errors in results, so that what we thought to be a fact may, on further inspection, turn out *not* to be a fact after all.

Nevertheless, Shroud researchers have been looking for more evidence to claim that the Shroud is much older than what the radiocarbon dating suggests. In 2005, Rogers stated emphatically, "Pyrolysis-mass-spectrometry results from the sample area coupled with microscopic and microchemical observations prove that the radiocarbon sample was not part of the original cloth of the Shroud of Turin. The radiocarbon date was thus not valid for determining the true age of the shroud."[169] In other words, it was not the technique of carbon dating itself that was questioned, but the origin of the sample used.

After applying false-color X-ray fluorescent photography, another researcher, Barrie Schwortz, a retired technical photographer and an Orthodox Jew, discovered that the sample taken displayed different chemical properties from the rest of the Shroud; it came from the only section of the cloth that showed up green. The conclusion rather obviously suggests that the side-strip sample does not represent the entire Shroud.[170]

Apparently, the radiocarbon sample had been dyed for restoration purposes. This was probably intended to make the color of the replacement material match the sepia color of the authentic

---

[169] Rogers, "Studies on the Radiocarbon Sample," 190.
[170] Barrie M. Schwortz, "Mapping of Research Test-Point Areas on the Shroud of Turin," *IEEE 1982 Proceedings of the International Conference on Cybernetics and Society* (1982): 538–547.

cloth. As mentioned earlier, the dye discovered on the sample was not manufactured until the late thirteenth century in Europe. Even then, it was not popularized for another hundred years.[171]

What should we learn from this? Science cannot prove or disprove anything with absolute certainty. There is so much that can go wrong in experimental testing, particularly before or during a carbon-dating test. It could very well be argued that the worst damage done to the Shroud did not come from fires, but from the radiocarbon-dating results published in 1988. Those results—dubious as they may be—made it very hard, even counter-scientific, in the minds of many, to claim that the Shroud must be much older than seven hundred years. You wonder, what is it about the Shroud of Turin that scares those scientists?

So we conclude that science does not have the last word on the Shroud, not even in carbon analysis, and religious faith continues to remain a significant part of the investigation.

[171] Hochberg, *Handspinner's Handbook*, 1–4.

9

Blood Analysis

As we saw already, the Shroud can easily be "contaminated" with pollen from different geographical areas and historical times, but contamination is very unlikely to happen with blood, unless the Shroud was touched by someone with an open wound. So, it's fair to assume that if there is blood on the Shroud, it must be from the person who was buried in the cloth. Then the obvious question for many, mostly skeptical, people is: Are the stains on the Shroud really blood, or are we dealing with the forgery of an incredibly talented artist?

The Image on the Shroud Is Not Painted

The Shroud seems to be littered by marks and stains, so how do we know these have not been created by paint or dye? It has become a rather popular belief lately, especially so after the radiocarbon test of 1988, that the Shroud is a hoax created by an exceptionally talented artist on a linen "canvas." At one point, the forgery story was breaking news. When you keep repeating news frequently and long enough, even if it's "fake news," it seems to become true in the minds of some, if not many.

Not surprisingly, the hypothesis of the Shroud as a painted linen keeps popping up repeatedly. Some have even gone wild in their fantasies. They find the painting so perfect that Leonardo da Vinci must have been the creator. One of their fanciest suggestions is that Leonardo soaked the Shroud in silver nitrate, placed it in a large camera obscura, and then photographed himself in the image. Didn't he also use his own face's proportions for his painting of the *Mona Lisa* (so the American artist Lillian F. Schwartz tells us)?[172] Well, the problem of her suggestion is that the first documented public exhibition of the Shroud of Turin occurred in 1355, almost a hundred years before Leonardo was even born!

What are we to make of claims like these? Well, one of the most notorious pitfalls of science is that scientists who come up with hypotheses—which are the engine of advancement in science, by the way—tend to equate hypothesizing with discovering. All that a scientist has come up with in a hypothesis is an invention conceived in his mind. There is a large step between that and making a qualified discovery. Scientists need evidence. The late Nobel laureate and physiologist Peter Medawar gave wise advice to a (young) scientist with his warning: "The intensity of the conviction that a hypothesis is true has no bearing on whether it is true or not."[173]

Well, the evidence for the painted-linen hypothesis is still missing. It is just an opinion, and opinions are not facts. To believe that the earth is flat does not make the earth flat. To believe that the Shroud is a painting does not make the Shroud a painting.

---

[172] Lillian F. Schwartz, "Lessons from Leonardo da Vinci: Additions to His Treatise on Computers and Art," *World Academy of Art and Science Proceedings* (1992).
[173] Ibid., 39.

Although science cannot conclusively prove or disprove that the Shroud is not a painting, it can provide us with at least some evidence to point one way or the other.

To find the evidence needed to dismiss the forgery hypothesis, the Shroud, under the supervision of several scientists, was observed with visible and ultraviolet spectrometry, infrared spectrometry, X-ray fluorescence spectrometry, and thermography. Fiber observations were made by pyrolysis-mass-spectrometry, Raman lasermicroprobe analyses, and microchemical testing. The outcome of these tests was quite convincing: no evidence for pigments or painting media was found.[174]

In 1978, technical photographer Barrie Schwortz was brought into the Shroud of Turin Research Project (STURP). Being a nonpracticing Jew, he expected to disprove the Shroud's authenticity and show it to be a painting from the Middle Ages. From his first moments of analysis, however, Schwortz began proving himself wrong. In his own words, "Thirty-seven years ago, when I went to Italy with STURP to examine the Shroud, I assumed it was a fake, some sort of medieval painting. But after 10 minutes studying it, I knew it was not [a painting]. As a professional photographer, I was looking for brush strokes. But there was no paint, and no brush strokes."[175]

There are many simple reasons why the image on the Shroud cannot possibly be painted. First, if it had been painted, there

---

[174] Raymond Rogers, "Image on Shroud of Turin Not Painted: Spectrometry-Fluorescence," Shroud of Turin Story, 2012, http://www.Bit.ly/RayRogers.

[175] Myra Kahn Adams, "Shroud of Turin: Interview with World's Leading Expert Who Happens to Be Jewish," interview with Barrie Schwortz, Townhall, March 8, 2020, https://www.bit.ly/BarrySchwortz.

would be an outline on the image, and there is none. Second, the image on the Shroud is only a few fibers deep, so the stains on the cloth are only superficial and do not cover the entire surface of the threads, which indicates they were not caused by using a paintbrush, for instance.[176] Third, the fibers on the cloth are not stuck together by any sort of paint or pigment. Fourth, the image of the man on the Shroud can be read by 3D imaging technology, but paintings fail this test.

The arguments against a painted image keep growing. Fifth, a painting cannot reflect something more than what the artist knew and wanted to convey; the Shroud, on the other hand, has too many details a painter could not have known. Sixth, the fire of 1532 would have caused cracking in the paint, yet there is none. Seventh, under ultraviolet light, the wounds display chemical particularities, such as serum clots, that can be found only in real blood; it is nearly impossible that a medieval artist would have a microscopic knowledge of the qualities of human blood. Eighth, it is almost impossible for a forger to apply blood to various regions on the Shroud during the short time blood takes to clot, ruling out the possibility of painting with real blood.[177] Ninth, the two parts of the Shroud that were cut and later stitched are hard to be made by a forger, who would have wanted to create a perfect relic of Jesus' burial cloth to show in public.

Furthermore, the Shroud is made of linen. Raw, unprepared linen repels water, which makes it difficult to cover with paint.

---

[176] Russ Breault, "Is the Shroud of Turin a Fake?," *EzineArticles. com*, October 11 2009.

[177] A. Adler. "The Orphaned Manuscript:, A Gathering of Publications on the Shroud of Turin," *Shroud Spectrum International*, special issue, 1st ed., ed. D. Crispino (Turin: Effata Editrice, 2002).

There is no such paint known that—applied to raw linen—would give the optical effect we see on the Turin Shroud.

Besides, the image is a photographic negative. When a traditional photograph is taken with a camera obscura, for instance, the image that should be the negative must appear as a positive image. If the Shroud is counterfeit, how would a medieval painter have been able to do that?[178]

Perhaps the most important argument against the painting hypothesis is that there is real blood on the Shroud, as I will show in the next section. In other words, the blood was on the Shroud first, and the image appeared later. "Blood first, image second" is a popular mantra of Shroud researchers. The only way to explain the phenomena is to accept that the man in the Shroud was indeed a crucified person, and thus possibly Jesus of Nazareth. Blood went on before the image, so there is no image beneath the blood.

The late Isabel Piczek, a Hungarian-born physicist and a professional artist, offers her own expert assessment:

> The Shroud was folded and refolded, rolled, exhibited, carried, exposed to sun and handled. All medieval convertible mediums require the use of a rigid support to paint on. The Shroud is not a rigid painting support. If a convertible paint medium would have been used on it, [then it] would have long ago lost its binding power, and medium and pigment would have fallen off as dust, destroying the image entirely. Whatever dust of either materials would have remained on its surface would have

---

[178] Although Leonardo da Vinci mentions the camera obscura in his *Codex Atlanticus*, the Shroud had been around long before.

to be dispersed all over the cloth and would not have accumulated logically in the image areas....

The artist cannot enlarge a smaller study made with a model to a life size scale and achieve what we see on the Shroud. The Shroud image shows details which can be further and further analyzed down to increasingly smaller areas and yet these details retain their lifelike integrity. The artist's smaller study enlarged to life-size shows a loss of details and becomes simplified and stylized.[179]

It has been argued, though, that some microscopic particles of paint were indeed detected on the Shroud. Oddly enough, these paint particles were not detected as *part* of the Shroud but rather *laid on top* of it. By studying fifty-two replicas of the holy cloth, Don Luigi Fossati, a Salesian of Don Bosco, explains that artists recreating the image customarily would lay their own creations over the original to "authenticate the copies."[180] Research archaeologist Paul Maloney thus also theorized that the paint particles found on the surface of the Shroud came from this "authenticating replicas" practice, verifying that the transfer of paint particles is possible in this manner.[181]

What may we conclude from all of this about the authenticity of the Shroud itself? A summary of STURP's conclusions

---

[179] Isabel Piczek, "Is the Shroud of Turin a Painting?" (summary of the material from her 1993 presentation at the Rome International Symposium on the Shroud), Shroud of Turin website, https://www.shroud.com/piczek.htm.

[180] Luigi Fossati, S.D.B., "Copies of the Holy Shroud," *Shroud Spectrum International*, no. 12 (September 1984), www.shroud.com/pdfs/ssi12part4.pdf.

[181] Paul Maloney, "Science, Archaeology, and the Shroud of Turin," *Approfondimento Sindone* 1 (1998): 75.

could not have said it more clearly: "No pigments, paints, dyes or stains have been found on the fibrils. X-ray, fluorescence and microchemistry on the fibrils preclude the possibility of paint being used as a method for creating the image."[182]

Are There Bloodstains on the Shroud?

Because there are many spots and stains on the Shroud, the question arises: How do we know that there are bloodstains among them?

The most common chemical tests used to determine the presence of blood involve a reaction with the ring structure of the blood protein hemoglobin, the presence of which was confirmed upon testing the Shroud's bloodstains. The tests also confirmed the presence of serum albumin, a blood protein made by the liver.[183] Further testing uncovered even more proteins and compounds in the Shroud that are present in human blood, including fibrin, fibrinogen, and bilirubin.[184] Besides, microchemical tests for proteins were positive in blood areas but negative in other parts of the Shroud.[185]

Alan Adler, a chemist, and John Heller, a physician, studied the blood flecks gathered on the sticky-tape samples of the Shroud image that the STURP team had brought back from Turin. They

---

[182] "A Summary of STURP's Conclusions."

[183] John Heller and Alan Adler, "Blood on the Shroud of Turin," *Applied Optics* 19, no. 16 (1980): 2742–2744.

[184] J. H. Heller, and A. Adler, "A Chemical Investigation of the Shroud of Turin," *Canadian Forensic Society Scientific Journal* 14 (1981): 81–103.

[185] Raymond N. Rogers, "Frequently Asked Questions" (2004), Shroud of Turin website, https://shroud.com/pdfs/rogers5faqs.pdf.

compared the samples with the spectra of blood spots and concluded that the blood on the Shroud is real. Adler reported:

> The tests we ran are more indicative than some of the tests that people routinely run. Some of the tests that people run for blood depend on the blood being fresh, the tests that I ran where we detected the so-called porphyrin is a test that does not depend on the blood being fresh, it is now being used more by people for the arch metric detection of blood. We actually found that you can accurately demonstrate 10,000 year-old blood using this particular test, which many of the more recent tests will not.[186]

It is worth noting that the blood particles revealed a high content of bilirubin, a breakdown product of the heme part of hemoglobin. This is significant for at least three reasons. First, it is a phenomenon revealing that the body has been subjected to extreme trauma. Second, an effect of this extreme trauma reflected by the bilirubin content is that the blood does not brown upon oxidization, as it usually does; instead, it remains bright red. This is exactly the color that the stains on the Shroud have. Third, Barbet, who had seen many bloodstains on cloth, noted that the Shroud's distinctive blood comprised "stains with clearly marked edges, which with such outstanding truthfulness reproduce the shape of the clots as they were formed naturally on the skin."[187] It is also worth noting that Giulio Fanti and his team discovered that the fibers of the bloodstains appeared to be covered with tiny particles containing creatinine and ferritin. These particles, or "nanoparticles," when found, did not indicate healthy blood,

---

[186] Heller and Adler, "Blood on the Shroud."
[187] Barbet, A Doctor at Calvary (Allegro), 33.

as they displayed irregular shapes, sizes, and distribution. They summarized their findings as follows:

TEM [transmission electron microscope] analyses show that the fiber is fully covered by creatinine nanoparticles.... Indeed, a high level of creatinine and ferritin is related to patients suffering of strong polytrauma like torture. Hence, the presence of these biological nanoparticles found during our TEM experiments point a violent death for the man wrapped in the Turin shroud.[188]

Whose Blood Is It?

Chemical tests can show us that there *is* blood in the stains on the Shroud, but they cannot tell us *whose* blood it is. That requires immunological tests, which are more specific than chemical.

Immunological testing is based on the fact that all cells in a person's body carry millions of molecules attached to their surfaces. These molecules are characteristic for the person who carries them. If the shape of those molecules is not "recognized" by the body as characteristic for this particular person, then the body prompts an immune response. This is where antigens and antibodies come in. *Antibodies* are proteins, so-called immunoglobulins, that are manufactured by the body to help fight against foreign substances called *antigens* (from the term "antibody generator"). When an antigen enters the body, it stimulates the immune system to produce specific antibodies.

The body's immunity response system works according to a lock-and-key model. It essentially says that molecules can

---

[188] Giulio Fanti et al., "Atomic Resolution Studies Detect New Biologic Evidences on the Turin Shroud," *PLoS ONE* 12, no. 6 (June 30, 2017).

"interact" with each other based on their shapes. Think of the way insulin works in the body. The lock is an insulin receptor molecule on the surface of a cell. This molecule keeps the gates to the cell closed. When the proper key, insulin in this case, is inserted into the "lock" of the cell, then the gate opens to let glucose from the blood enter the cell.

The lock-and-key mechanism also works for other situations in the body—for example, the interaction between antigens and antibodies.[189] Certain antibodies fit like "keys" into the specific "locks" of antigens, so to speak. It's a tight fit; smaller keys, larger keys, or incorrectly shaped keys do not fit into the lock; only the correctly shaped one opens its corresponding lock. Because of their fit, antibodies and antigens can form complexes that clump together and then can be removed by other blood cells in the body. In this case, the antibody unlocks the "gate" to a series of destructive actions that eliminate the foreign antigen.

This mechanism of lock-and-key can also explain what happens during wrong blood transfusions. Red blood cells have molecules that stick out on the surface of the cell. If those molecules are not recognized by the body, then they act like antigens that activate the production of antibodies, meaning that they activate an attack response. The lock-and-key model explains why only certain antibodies, the "keys," can bind with certain antigens, the "locks," and thus "recognize" them. Because molecules not recognized by an individual are interpreted as foreign entities, persons with certain blood types usually contain in their circulation specific antibodies that react

---

[189] B.C. Braden et al., "Protein Motion and Lock and Key Complementarity in Antigen-Antibody Reactions," *Pharmaceutica Acta Helvetiae* 69, no. 4 (1995): 225–230.

with the antigens they themselves lack on the surface of their own red blood cells.

There are, in fact, more than twenty blood antibody-antigen groupings, but out of the twenty, the ABO system is used most frequently, due to its importance in blood transfusions. In this system, there are four fundamental blood types: A, B, AB, and O. The blood types distinguish the types of molecules carried on a person's red blood cells. Type A blood indicates the presence of A molecules; type B indicates B molecules; type AB carries both; and type O carries neither.[190]

Since persons with blood type O, for instance, have neither the A nor the B molecule on their red blood cells, blood cells carrying either A or B molecules act like antigens, generating the production of antibodies, when entering the blood of the receiver. Incompatible blood transfusions are the result of exposure to incompatible blood types. Type A blood is incompatible with type B because they each produce antibodies that attack the foreign molecule; A fights off anti-A, and B fights off anti-B. Incompatibility triggers agglutination, or clumping in the blood, which can cause serious harm to one's health. This reaction is what makes people with the O type of blood so vulnerable during transfusion; they can receive only type O blood without triggering an attack response. On the other hand, it is an "easy" type of blood to receive because it carries none of the antigens that would activate responses in the other blood types.

How can this knowledge be used to determine the blood type of the person buried in the Shroud of Turin? Determining the blood type of a person is called "blood typing." This can be done

---

[190] "O" is derived from the word *Ohne*, the German word for "without," for they have no ABO molecules on their cells.

in two ways—either with "forward typing" or with "reverse typing." *Forward* typing is searching for type A and B antigens on red blood cells. *Reverse* typing is looking for naturally occurring anti-A and anti-B antibodies in the blood serum. There are a few problems we may have to face, however.

First, when blood has left the body and the aging process begins, the blood oxidizes, dehydrates, and falls apart with time, making it harder and harder to study. Remarkably, though, the blood on the Shroud is rather well preserved, due perhaps to the protecting presence of aloes and myrrh.

Second, many factors can lead to errors in determining the blood group of ancient stains. A whole series of antigens of animals, worms, and bacteria are known to produce false-positive responses. Kelly P. Kearse, who studied immunology at Johns Hopkins University and was a principal investigator at the National Institutes of Health, warns us of such responses: "False positives from antigens present on contaminating bacteria, fungi and insects is [sic] the main objection to the validity of blood typing studies done on the Shroud."[191] False positives from such contaminating antigens are the main reason blood-typing studies done on the Shroud can be questioned. Kearse also reported, however, that "colorless fibers taken from the bed of the bloodstain gave no response with anti-A or anti-B antibodies indicating that any contaminating false positive antigens cannot be widespread."[192]

Third, the old blood samples must retain their distinguishing blood-group antibodies in order for them to be categorized

---

[191] Kelly P. Kearse, "Blood on the Shroud of Turin: An Immunological Review" (2012): 11, Shroud of Turin website, https://www.shroud.com/pdfs/kearse.pdf.

[192] Ibid., 12.

properly. What's even more unlikely, yet even more important, is that the three-dimensional shape of the antigen-binding "key" is sufficiently intact to function correctly. However, as Kearse reports, "When bloodstained Shroud fibers were evaluated by this method, no anti-A or anti-B antibodies were detected."[193] This might indicate that the person buried in the Shroud had blood type AB, but not necessarily so because A and B antibodies may have been there but are no longer intact.

Fourth, because animals contain ABO molecules on their red blood cells as well, more advanced testing is required to distinguish it from human blood. In 2010, such a test was developed to identify glycophorin A, a protein carried on the surfaces of red blood cells in humans, but unfortunately, it is also carried in other primates. It is worth noting, however, that finding blood from other primates on the Shroud is extremely unlikely, unless it was used by a forger.

Despite these possible problems, there have been specific positive results for blood typing on the Shroud of Turin. In the early 1980s, Pier Luigi Baima Bollone and a team of scientists uncovered evidence that the blood found on the cloth was type AB.[194] This blood type is rare—about 3 percent of the world population—but has a surprisingly high frequency in Palestine. The evidence was not definitive, however, as older blood samples have a higher likelihood of showing type AB—the older blood gets, the more of its antibodies are lost, meaning that any blood type, over time, would eventually look like type AB.[195]

---

[193] Kearse, "Blood on the Shroud," 12.

[194] P.L. Baima Bollone, "The Forensic Characteristics of the Blood Marks in the Turin Shroud: Past, Present, and Future," *Int. 14 Scientific Symposium* (Turin: Effata Editrice, 2000), 125–135.

[195] Wilson and Schwortz, *The Turin Shroud*, 77.

To rule out the possibility of nonhuman blood on the Shroud, Bollone searched for more distinguishing antigens found on red blood cells, namely M, N, and S antigens. After performing a series of serological tests, the researchers reported the blood on the Shroud to be type MNS.[196] The presence of the S antigen proved most significant, as it is carried only by humans and not by other primates. Upon observing Bollone's results, Kearse concludes, "Given that unstained fibers showed no reactivity, it is valid to conclude that bloodstained fibers contain both N and S antigens. Moreover, since the S antigen has no counterpart in primates or other animals, these results support the conclusion that the blood on the Shroud is of human origin."[197]

Obviously, this does not answer the question of whose blood it is that we find on the Shroud. Even if we know it is from someone who has AB and MNS blood, that does not mean it is the blood of Jesus because we don't know Jesus' blood type to begin with. Even if we did, it wouldn't prove that the Shroud has Jesus' blood on it. As we said before, science cannot prove much — nor can it disprove much; it can only make things more likely or less likely.

We could also turn the tables and ask ourselves why we care about blood types when it comes to the Shroud. Such interest seems to be mainly based on curiosity among scholars and scientists. But there is a more important reason: we want to authenticate the Shroud of Turin as best as we can; otherwise it would become just another ancient cloth, an antiquity. To merit our real attention, we want to know that this unique cloth is marked

---

[196] P. L. Baima Bollone et al., "Ricerca degli antigeni M, N ed S nelle trace di sangue sulla Sindone," *Sindon* 34 (1985): 9–13.

[197] Kearse, "Blood on the Shroud," 14.

with real blood from a real person, from someone who, in the words of the Apostles' Creed, "suffered under Pontius Pilate, was crucified, died, and was buried." Once we know that's true, the specific blood type is only of secondary concern.

Only then are we permitted to claim in faith that the Shroud does carry Jesus' blood, in light of all the other indications we have seen thus far. Faith and science each have their own input and are not really in conflict with each other. We still have strong indications, coming both from science and faith, that we are dealing with a cloth in which a person was buried—Jesus of Nazareth, our Lord and Savior. This very well might make us wonder: Has Jesus really left behind for us an image of Himself?

So we must come to the conclusion that science does not have the last word, not even in blood analysis, when it comes to the Shroud of Turin. Yet it should not contradict what faith tells us and may even confirm what we know based on faith. Religious faith may add new elements and insights that are beyond the scope of the blood analysis done by science.

10

DNA Analysis

Not too long ago, there was even more "breaking news" about the Shroud of Turin. This time, the news came from the History Channel and was promoted all over the media. It was announced and summarized as follows:

> Now for the first time in history a man of faith and a man of science are teaming up to search for Jesus' DNA. Using the latest advances in DNA technology Oxford University geneticist George Busby and biblical scholar Pastor Joe Basile are investigating the world's most famous holy relics including the Shroud of Turin, the Sudarium of Oviedo and the newly discovered bones of Jesus' cousin, John the Baptist. Their journey takes them to holy sites around the world from Spain and Italy to Israel and the shores of the Black Sea. By extracting and analyzing samples of each of these holy relics they hope to retrieve a sample of DNA that possibly belongs to Jesus or a member of his family. They believe that if they can find a strand of Jesus' DNA it could help identify who among us today are descendants of Jesus and provide us with new insight into the man many consider to be the most important person in history, Jesus.

The two researchers, a geneticist and a Protestant pastor, claimed to have found that Jesus' maternal ancestors came from the Druze population in the Near East; that Jesus' DNA was very similar to the DNA of his cousin John the Baptist; that Jesus had brothers and sisters; and that Jesus even had descendants of His own.

What are we to make of all of this? What is true, what is possibly true, and what is impossibly true? Let's find out with the help of DNA analysis.

Blood DNA from the Shroud

DNA that is found in the nucleus of the cell is called nuclear DNA. It is packaged in chromosomes during a certain time of the cell cycle. Structurally, DNA consists of four bases, called nucleotides, which are symbolized by the letters A, T, C, and G. These four bases are the building blocks of DNA. Some DNA parts are "coding DNA," which contain the genes that code for various proteins, including enzymes, that are needed for the body's structure and metabolism. Currently, it seems reasonable to say that the number of protein-coding genes has been lowered to around 21,000 — which is only a little bit more than the 20,470 genes a tiny roundworm needs to manufacture its utter simplicity.

Geneticists can use "coding DNA" to determine the different forms a particular gene can harbor. Each individual can only carry up to two forms of a gene — one coming from the father and the other coming from the mother. For example, the gene for the ABO blood group system may have two forms of the gene (AB, AO, or BO), or just two of the same form (AA or BB or OO). However, genes may have many more forms than the two found in one individual. Thanks to differences like these, it may be possible to compare individuals with each other based on their genetic differences.

How does all of this relate to the DNA analysis of the Shroud of Turin? A study performed in the late 1990s discovered the presence of human DNA on the Shroud. One of the study's microbiologists, Leoncio Garza-Valdes, reported that he had sequenced portions of three genes from threads taken from Shroud bloodstains.[198] Kearse explains which genes were analyzed: "the beta-globin gene (a subunit of hemoglobin), and the amelogenin X and amelogenin Y genes, present on X and Y chromosomes, respectively. The threads examined were from the left-hand area and the occipital region (the back of the head)."[199] Garza-Valdes concluded from his findings that "all three segments of human genes tested were positive, indicating the blood of the man on the Shroud came from a human male."[200]

But from which part of the blood does this information come? The irony is that DNA, including hemoglobin DNA, can be found in every cell of the body other than mature red blood cells. In mammals — including humans — red blood cells contain DNA only in their early stages of development. The DNA is present in the cell's nucleus, which is shed by the time the red blood cell reaches maturity and enters the bloodstream. This fact means that any DNA found on the Shroud would necessarily come from white blood cells present in the body's immune system (such as

---

[198] L. Garza-Valdes, *The DNA of God?* (New York: Doubleday, 1999).

[199] Kelly P. Kearse, "DNA Analysis and the Shroud of Turin: Development of a Shroud CODIS," 12, Shroud of Turin website, https://www.shroud.com/pdfs/kearse3.pdf.

[200] Garza-Valdes, *The DNA of God?*, 39.

lymphocytes, neutrophils, and macrophages). But that does not necessarily invalidate the claims made above.

Is there more to report on DNA analysis? Rather recent developments in DNA research and DNA technology have opened the door for more discriminating information about the DNA of individuals. Recently, it has been determined that DNA contains a huge amount of so-called noncoding DNA, in addition to protein-coding DNA. Some of this DNA is repetitive DNA, harboring large numbers of short repetitive DNA sequences—so-called short tandem repeats, or STRs. They are scattered throughout the DNA in the cell nucleus. Whereas only about 1.5 percent of the human nuclear DNA seems to code for proteins, the rest consists of regulatory sections and noncoding DNA, including STRs.

To differentiate between individuals, the part of DNA that codes for proteins would be rather limited because those proteins cannot vary too much without affecting their vitality. STRs, on the other hand, are highly variable regions in the noncoding DNA, which makes them more suitable for identification of individuals. The greater the number of STR sequences that are examined, the more discriminatory power they have in determining the genetic relationship of samples under investigation.

Has all of this had an impact on research regarding the Shroud of Turin? Not quite. The main reason is that most developments in this field are rather recent and depend on specific conditions. They require very advanced techniques to extract and analyze DNA. Granted, some advances have been made, but they are not spectacular.[201]

---

[201] A good, well-documented overview was given by Kelly Kearse, who points out the caveats that need to be made, in his article

Besides, there are at least two main obstacles in DNA analysis: fragmentation and contamination. Let's start with fragmentation. The DNA found on the Shroud could very well be two thousand years old. DNA degrades over time and is broken down into smaller and smaller parts. All DNA studies of the Shroud report badly fragmented DNA.

Fortunately, fragmentation is not the biggest hurdle for DNA research on the Shroud of Turin. Nowadays, we have techniques to multiply even small DNA fragments into numerous copies, making it possible to study them better. One of these techniques is the *polymerase chain reaction* (PCR), which is a method widely used in molecular biology to make millions to billions of copies of a specific DNA sample rapidly, thus allowing scientists to take a very small sample of DNA and amplify it to an amount large enough to study in detail. PCR is a powerful and fast tool that can create almost a billion DNA copies in just three hours.

Here is Kearse's assessment of this technique:

> PCR is most efficient at copying DNA fragments that are at least 80 bases in length, which could be problematic for certain aged DNA that might exist in smaller pieces. Next generation sequencers are able to read each base separately, which has made analysis of many ancient DNA genomes (often isolated in small fragments) now possible.... In addition, modified DNA sequencing methods are currently available that aid in study of highly fragmented and degraded DNA, based on analysis

"DNA Analysis and the Shroud of Turin: Development of a Shroud CODIS."

of mini-STRs combined with single nucleotide polymorphisms (SNPs).[202]

In addition to fragmentation, there is another hurdle for DNA analysis: contamination. There are various sources of contamination. First of all, there is always the possibility of operator contamination—that is, through people who handle the sample and then leave their own DNA traces behind. In the hopes of reducing such contamination, Kearse wisely recommends that "[for] serious study, it would be worth considering that a DNA sample, coming from a simple cheek swab, be submitted by all those who handle the DNA sample." Thus, this form of contamination can be reduced by analyzing the DNA of the operators and comparing their profile with the profiles found on the sample they are studying.

Second, there is contamination by all the people who have touched the Shroud of Turin in its long history. The risk of contamination is much higher with DNA analysis than it is with blood analysis. Unlike blood, DNA is in almost all body cells, including skin cells. Blood analysis can be contaminated only by foreign blood, while DNA analysis can be contaminated by nearly any foreign cell. Therefore, even the mere touch of an object such as the Shroud can easily contaminate the samples taken from it.

This "touch DNA" makes up a significantly complicating factor. Humans lose around four hundred thousand skin cells per day, meaning that DNA from countless individuals may be present on the Shroud of Turin. Besides, given the fact that the Shroud was displayed and handled for over hundreds of years by untold

---

[202] Kearse, "DNA Analysis," 8.

numbers of people, contaminating DNA is to be expected—not to mention the possible contamination from the many restoration procedures and scientific tests that have occurred since.

Is there a way to find out whether the DNA under examination is foreign? Ideally, there would be, if we were able to distinguish DNA from blood cells versus DNA from skin cells that came through contamination. Theoretically, it should be possible to differentiate between these two sources, but I am not aware of any attempts that have been made for the Shroud itself.

The Mother of the Man in the Shroud

DNA is present not only in the cell's nucleus but also in its mitochondria, which is the energy provider of the cell. This DNA is called *mtDNA*. Red blood cells have no nucleus after they mature and enter the bloodstream, meaning they no longer have nuclear DNA, but they still have mitochondrial DNA.

What is so different and important about mtDNA in comparison with nuclear DNA? Nuclear DNA perhaps gains more attention because it is significantly larger. Compared with nuclear DNA, mtDNA is much smaller, containing only thirty-seven genes in total in the form of an enclosed loop. Though different in sizing, however, both types are composed of the same building blocks (the bases A, T, C, and G).

Another important difference is that a cell has only one nucleus, whereas there are hundreds to thousands of mitochondria present in each cell, and each mitochondrion can contain several copies of mtDNA. There may be one or two copies of nuclear DNA in a cell but between one hundred and ten thousand copies of mtDNA, making it highly useful when nuclear DNA is missing, damaged, or, in this case, aged.

In addition to location, size, and number, the two types of DNA differ in the means by which they are passed from generation to generation. Whereas nuclear DNA is passed along from both parents, mtDNA only comes from the mother. Although males do carry mtDNA, they do not transmit it to offspring. During intercourse and conception, male mitochondria are stored only in the tail of the male sperm cells; female mitochondria are stored inside the female egg cell itself and immediately become part of the zygote upon fertilization. Because mitochondrial DNA does not get "reshuffled," as nuclear DNA does, mtDNA is passed unmixed from mothers to children, along the maternal line. What follows from this is that mtDNA on the Shroud can tell us something about the mother of the person buried in the Shroud and about the mother of that mother and so on back in time.

Furthermore, the high mutation rate of mtDNA emphasizes the possible parental link between different individuals. The mtDNA sequences vary widely from person to person and will never be identical, unless they share a mother. This means that two samples that share few or no sequences are not connected through the maternal line, whereas those samples that are relatively close might indeed be connected.

There is one more thing that needs to be explained before we can arrive at the point: mtDNA can be tested for so-called single-nucleotide polymorphisms (SNPs), which are single base pair changes in the DNA. Any specific inherited SNP in mtDNA sections creates a "DNA signature" (*haplotype*). Since SNPs can last through many generations, they can be used as markers to trace an individual's maternal ancestry. A group of individuals who share similar haplotypes is known as a *haplogroup*, identified by certain DNA markers of rare mutations in mtDNA segments.

All individuals in a given haplogroup have a common ancestor at some point back in time. Each haplogroup can then further split into subgroups characterized by some additional mutation markers.

Think of this example: if we would use letters to represent certain markers in the following simple case, we could assume that haplotype ABCDE is the maternal ancestor of both haplotype aBCDE and haplotype ABCDe, which had two different mutations—and together they would form a haplogroup. If enough individuals are examined for their haplotypes, maps can be created, showing the distribution of various haplogroups across the world.

With his team of experts at the University of Padua in Italy, the geneticist Gianni Barcaccia applied this information to the Shroud of Turin. The team used a set of dust particles vacuumed from the Shroud which had been donated by Giulio Fanti in 2010 after having received them from Giovanni Riggi di Numana in 2006.[203]

The team found representatives of diverse haplogroups on the Shroud. In their own words:

> Some haplogroups are widespread, while others are geographically and ethnically more localized.... For instance, haplogroup H1 is very common in Western Europe, with a frequency peak among Iberians (~ 25%) but also among the populations of Northwestern Africa, including the Berbers. Haplogroup H4 is instead present at low and rather similar frequencies in Western (Iberia ~ 3%) and

---

[203] G. Fanti and P. Malfi, *Sindone: primo secolo dopo Cristo* (Udine, Italy: Edizioni Segno, 2014), 403.

Eastern Europe (~ 1%), the Caucasus (~ 3%) and the Near East (~ 1%). Haplogroup H33 is rare and mainly found thus far among the Druze, a minority population of Israel, Jordan, Lebanon, and Syria.[204]

Barcaccia and his team came to the following conclusion:

Individuals from different ethnic groups and geographical locations came into contact with the Shroud either in Europe (France and Turin) or directly in their own lands of origin (Europe, northeast Africa, Caucasus, Anatolia, Middle East and India).... We cannot say anything more on its origin.[205]

It is worth mentioning that each of the three scientists working directly with the Shroud samples had provided sequenced samples of their own mtDNA so as to eliminate the possibility of operator contamination.

Obviously, it is unwarranted for geneticist Busby and biblical scholar Joe Basile to claim that the Mother of Jesus was of Druze origin, especially considering the sheer number of contaminating DNA particles that likely exists on the Shroud through centuries of veneration and travel. Beyond common sense, Barcaccia and his team had proven as much. The Shroud had made a long journey—secretly carried from Judea in AD 30 or 33; housed in Edessa, Turkey, and then in Constantinople; smuggled to safety in Athens, Greece; carried across the Alps to France; and then finally ending up in Italy.

---

[204] Gianni Barcaccia et al., "Uncovering the sources of DNA found on the Turin Shroud," *Nature, Scientific Reports* 5, no. 14484 (2015): 4.

[205] Ibid., 2.

To pick out of this huge diversity the haplogroup H33, characteristic for people of Druze origin, is rather arbitrary. Besides, it's not surprising that this particular haplogroup could have left its traces behind because the Shroud may very well have gone through Druze territory on its way to Edessa. Some of the first followers of Jesus in Galilee may have been of ethnic Druze origin. When we think of the Druze population nowadays, we assume they are Muslims, but they couldn't have joined the religion of Islam before Mohammed came along in the seventh century.

Although the Druze religion officially began in the eleventh century, oral tradition reveals that the Druze line, made up of multiple ethnic groups, dates back thousands of years. This history is also reflected in their mtDNA, as suggested both in and beyond haplogroup H33. Researchers at the Technion-Israel Institute of Technology found out that "the Druze harbor a remarkable diversity of mtDNA types that appear to have separated from each other many thousands of years ago."[206]

George Busby even went as far as comparing the mtDNA profile found on the Shroud with the mtDNA profile discovered on the bones presumed to be of John the Baptist, a first cousin of Jesus. However, as was uncovered later, the DNA sequence he had come up with matched the person who had extracted the bone material—meaning that it was more than likely to be a case of operator contamination. DNA analysis is a minefield, and the Druze connection claimed by Busby might very well be blasted therein.

What remains standing is this: DNA analysis of the mtDNA of the person on the Shroud, presumably Jesus, opens for us a

[206] American Technion Society, "Genetics Confirm Oral Traditions of Druze in Israel," *ScienceDaily*, May 12, 2008, https://www.sciencedaily.com/releases/2008/05/080508182219.htm.

window into the mtDNA of his mother, presumably Mary, and thus of her mother, presumably St. Anne, and so forth back in time. But what does this do for us?

The Mother of Jesus

There is a common assumption, even among Christians, especially from the Protestant churches, including Pastor Basile's, that Jesus had brothers and sisters. They happily quote Mark 6:3, for instance: "Is he not ... the brother of James and Joses and Judas and Simon?" Many similar statements have been made by those who claim to be Scripture scholars. Sometimes, following the work of Scripture scholars can lead us into disbelief, but in these cases, it should be pinpointed to disbelief in Scripture scholars, rather than in Scripture itself.

Nevertheless, the idea that Jesus had brothers and sisters is a widespread and faulty assumption. This probably goes back to the fact that those who hold this idea have an uneasy relationship with Mary, the Mother of Jesus. The truth is this: in Aramaic, the language that Jesus and most of His followers spoke, as in biblical Hebrew, there is no word for "cousins." The words "brother" and "sister" can include cousins, relatives, and even members of the Christian community later on in Church history. We find the term "brother" already used in this broad sense in the Old Testament, referring to a wide variety of people—any human being,[207] a neighbor,[208] a kinsman,[209] a friend,[210] or simply an ally.[211] It is

---

[207] Gen. 9:25; 19:7; Exod. 32:27, 29.
[208] Lev. 19:17.
[209] Deut. 23:7–8; Jer. 34:9.
[210] 2 Sam. 1:26.
[211] Amos 1:9.

somewhat similar to the currently colloquial use of the word "guys" in the United States, which can refer to both men and women, and both adults and children.

Something similar can be said about the term "sister." When Mary was standing under the Cross of her Son, she was accompanied by her "sister" Mary. In the words of St. John: "standing by the cross of Jesus were his mother, and his mother's sister, Mary the wife of Clopas, and Mary Magdalene."[212] It is quite silly to think that Mary's mother would have called two of her daughters by the same name, Mary. In other words, Mary of Clopas is not a "sister" in our sense of the word; she is just a relative, most likely a first cousin.

St. Jerome, who translated the Vulgate from Hebrew and Greek into Latin, was very aware of this. He explained in 383 that Jesus' "brothers," as mentioned in the Bible, were actually His cousins, since in Jewish idiom, cousins were also referred to as "brothers."[213] Jerome also knew that Jesus was the only child of Mary and Joseph—and he is certainly not alone in thinking this. In addition to Sacred Tradition—the teaching of Jesus Christ handed on to the Church through the apostles and their successors, in particular the Church Fathers—there are many indications in the Bible that Mary did not have any other children. The people of Nazareth, for instance, referred to Jesus as "*the* [ὁ in Greek] son of Mary,"[214] not "*a* son of Mary." That's why Jesus, hanging on the Cross, could ask the apostle John to take care of Mary,[215] as she had no other children to do so for her; otherwise

---

[212] John 19:25.
[213] Jerome, *The Perpetual Virginity of Blessed Mary*, 16, New Advent, https://www.newadvent.org/fathers/3007.htm.
[214] Mark 6:3.
[215] John 19:26.

this request would be a serious offense against any other living children of hers.

The fact that Jesus is called her "firstborn son"[216] does not imply that Mary had other, younger sons, born after the firstborn. If that were the case, we could not call a child "firstborn" until other children had been born. Jesus is brought to the Temple in accordance with Jewish Law: "The Lord said to Moses, 'Consecrate to me all the first-born; whatever is the first to open the womb among the people of Israel, both of man and of beast, is mine.'"[217] One does not have to wait for this until a second child is born. Instead, the term "firstborn" conveys a legal message, associated with special privileges in Jewish law. St. Jerome said, "By first-born we understand not only one who is succeeded by others, but one who has had no predecessor.... First-born is a title of him who opens the womb and is not to be restricted to him who has brothers."[218]

Do we know more details about Mary's genealogy? Not really, at least not at first sight. The Gospels tell us about St. Joseph's genealogy, tracing him back to David. Roy Schoeman, a Catholic convert from Judaism, could not have said it more clearly: "The New Covenant is a covenant through faith.... In contrast to this, the Old Covenant is a covenant through blood, through descent, through membership in the genealogical clan that began with Abraham's son Isaac.... Being a Jew is to be born into the Jewish community."[219] As the prophecy says, "There shall come forth a shoot from the stump of Jesse [the father of King David], and a branch shall grow out of his roots."[220]

---

[216] Luke 2:7.
[217] Exod. 13:1–2.
[218] Jerome, *The Perpetual Virginity*, 12.
[219] Schoeman, *Salvation Is from the Jews*, 64.
[220] Isa. 11:1–2.

Joseph's genealogy cannot really be the genealogy of Jesus, however, for the simple reason that Jesus was not Joseph's biological son. Instead, it is Mary's genealogy that's important for Jesus' ancestry. But what do we know about Mary's ancestors? From Luke's narrative on the Roman census, we can predict that Mary and Joseph came from the same tribe.[221] St. Thomas Aquinas says something similar: "If Joachim, Mary's father, was of the family of Aaron ... then we must believe that Joachim's mother, or else his wife, was of the family of David, so long as we say that Mary was in some way descended from David,"[222] and if Mary was descended from David, then so was Jesus.

In other words, Joseph and Mary were relatives, both belonging to the tribe of Judah, being descendants of David. This line of ancestry means that Christ, fulfilling the Old Testament prophecy, came from the line of David both according to the law, through Joseph, and according to blood, through Mary. Joseph Ratzinger, later Pope Benedict XVI, put it this way: "Joseph is the 'legal' father of Jesus. Through him, Jesus belongs by law, 'legally,' to the house of David. And yet, he comes from elsewhere, 'from above' — from God himself."[223]

It is interesting to note in this context that the Talmudic Rabbis (AD 200–500) used to speak of two Messiahs.[224] The first, *Messiah ben Joseph*, will suffer and die. The second, *Messiah ben David*, will be a king who leads his people to victory. In the New Testament, Jesus was literally known as "Jesus the son of

---

[221] Luke 2:3–5.

[222] Thomas Aquinas, *Summa Theologica*, III, q. 31, art. 2, ad. 1.

[223] Joseph Ratzinger (Pope Benedict XVI), *Jesus of Nazareth: The Infancy Narratives* (New York: Image Books, 2012), 7.

[224] Schoeman, *Salvation Is from the Jews*, 119.

Joseph."[225] Not only was He going to suffer and die, but He will also ultimately lead His people to victory as *Messiah ben David*. If the Shroud of Turin is indeed the Shroud of Jesus, then we have evidence that *Messiah ben Joseph* did suffer and die, so that He could lead us to our final victory as *Messiah ben David*.

A Virgin Birth?

The only puzzling part of all of this is that Jesus was born to a virgin according to Scriptures. After all we have seen about the man in the Shroud of Turin, we will naturally wonder as to how the man in the Shroud—presumably Jesus, the Son of Mary—could have a Y chromosome if Mary was a virgin. How could that be with genetics telling us that the Y chromosome *must* come from a biological father that Jesus did not have?

Yet genetic research on the Shroud tells us that the man buried in the cloth did have a Y chromosome. After examining two blood samples taken from the cloth at the back of the head, Victor Tryon of the University of Texas found human DNA from both X and Y chromosomes, confirming that the Shroud's blood came from a human male.[226] Tryon did find that the DNA was very degraded, but this is to be expected with ancient DNA.[227]

Many have tried to reconcile genetics with what the Bible tells us. In trying to do so, they have come up with some bizarre scenarios. Here are a few of the theories:

---

[225] At the time, Jews used a patronymic rather than a family name.
[226] Elvio Carlino et al., "Atomic Resolution Studies Detect New Biologic Evidences on the Turin Shroud," *PLoS ONE* 12, no. 6.
[227] Garza-Valdes, *The DNA of God?*, 41–42.

• Mary may have had testicular feminization, meaning that she carried the male Y chromosome while maintaining the bodily appearance of a female. This genetic mutation occurs due to an irregularity in the X chromosome, in which it fails to respond to male hormones. But even if this were the case, a second extremely unlikely event—a reversal mutation—would have to have taken place for Jesus to be (and appear as) a male. Really?

• Another case presents XY gonadal dysgenesis as a possible explanation. People with this mutation, called Swyer syndrome, can be born with female external genitalia and underdeveloped ovaries or testes. This means they have sex glands that do not work, caused by a defect in the SRY gene on chromosome Y. Could Jesus really be someone like that?

• Jesus may have had two X chromosomes. However, since He was clearly male, He must have had the SRY gene, usually found on the Y chromosome, which acts like a master switch and triggers the development of a male. But the SRY gene, instead of being in the Y chromosome, must have been inserted into a location where it is not normally found: the X chromosome. In this scenario, Jesus would have been an XX-male generated by an SRY inserted into an X chromosome.

Why are these hypotheses not worth much attention? They use, or rather abuse, science to create an awkward image of either Jesus or Mary, or both. Why does that not work? The reason for this is simple: what these trials are trying to achieve is mixing science and religion into a single amalgam. The apparent result, however, is like a mixture of oil and water—two components that do not mix well. As I said at the beginning, there are questions that science cannot answer, as there are questions that religion cannot answer. Therefore, religious issues cannot be solved by science, and scientific issues cannot be solved by religion. They each have their own authority and their own limitations.

Science can tell us that Jesus was a man with a Y chromosome, but the issue of how the Word became flesh is not a scientific one. The Incarnation of the God-Man through the Virgin Birth is beyond the reach of science, and a bizarre concoction of science and religion to explain religious mysteries is bound to fail. Just as the presence of the human soul cannot be found in skulls or fossils, so the existence of the Virgin Birth cannot be found in chromosomes and genes. Thinking differently creates a concoction of two different entities.

Only people who believe science to be their all-powerful, all-knowing god expect that all our questions can be answered by science. But science does not have that power of omnicompetence; this thinking is a widespread myth born out of the Enlightenment era. It is in fact a totalitarian ideology, for it allows no room for anything but itself. Unfortunately, many of us have been infected by the virus of scientism—the idea that all our questions must have scientific answers—but, in itself, it is merely an idea, certainly not a scientific discovery based on experiments. We will discuss scientism more in the next chapter.

The fact of the matter is that there are so many questions in life that science cannot answer. The question of the Virgin Birth of Jesus is just one of them. Science simply cannot explain it; the mystery lies beyond its expertise. Not all questions about Jesus can be answered and solved by genetics, for instance. It is like expecting DNA to tell us the square root of four. Fortunately, there is much more to Jesus than His DNA: He is the Messiah, the God-Man, the Son of God.

Science and religion both have their own authority and expertise. In the world of science, we can find only atoms, molecules, nucleotides, genes, cells, brains, and the like, but no souls, no sins, no angels, no miracles, no redemption. Science cannot find out, for instance, whether human beings have souls, for the soul is immaterial. Science cannot find out whether Jesus is the Son of God, for God is not a scientific hypothesis.[228] On the other hand, religion has its own limitations too: it cannot find out whether radiocarbon dating is reliable, or whether there is real human blood in the stains of the Shroud. Science and religion each have their own "territory" and their own authority.

This authoritative divide has consequences for both sides. Because science has its own authority and expertise, religion should stay away from scientific issues. Something similar is also true of science. Because religion has its own authority and expertise, science should respect matters of religious belief. Science can tell us that Jesus was a male with a Y chromosome, but it cannot tell us that He is divine and born of a virgin. Science and religion both have their own questions and their own answers, and as the saying goes, good fences make good neighbors.

There are two sides to the story here. On the one hand, if the Shroud of Turin is indeed the Shroud of Jesus, then the Shroud tells us that Jesus did have a Y chromosome, so He was fully human, fully male, which would be in complete accordance with what the Catholic Faith tells us: Jesus, though God, was fully human, fully male: He was the God-Man. This concerns the human part of His birth of the Virgin Mary.

---

[228] Gerard Verschuuren, *A Catholic Scientist Proves God Exists* (Manchester, NH: Sophia Institute Press, 2020).

Dr. Taylor Marshall adds to this:

> Now then, the Catholic Church has condemned the heresy of Valentinus who wrongly taught that Our Lord Jesus Christ did not take genetic material from Mary, but rather passed through her "like water through a straw." The heresy of Valentinus wrongly taught that Mary was merely an incubator of Christ, but not His true mother.... We know from Catholic magisterial teaching that Christ acquired his genetic material from Mary. He was derived from her human substance and [she] was truly His mother and thus the Mother of God."[229]

As St. Thomas Aquinas put it, "The Blessed Virgin was not Christ's Father, but His Mother.[230]

On the other hand, there is also a divine part to the Virgin Birth—the birth of the God-Man. So, St. Joseph was Jesus' father according to the law but not according to the flesh. Why is the Virgin Birth of Jesus so important to the Catholic Faith? Because it gave Jesus the "status" of divinity! If Jesus, in His full humanity, was not divine at the same time, His suffering, Crucifixion, and death would have been worthless and insignificant. Had Jesus not been *divine*, He would have been only a prophet at best, and the whole economy of salvation would be up for grabs. No mere man can take away all the sins of the world[231]—only a God-Man can. St. Proclus of Constantinople

---

[229] Dr. Taylor Marshall, "Is Jesus Christ the 'Genetic Twin' of the Blessed Virgin Mary? Let's ask St Thomas Aquinas," Dr. Taylor Marshall, https://taylormarshall.com/2013/02/is-jesus-christ-genetic-twin-of-blessed.html.

[230] Thomas Aquinas, *Summa Theologica*, III, q. 32, art. 4.

[231] See John 1:29.

said in the year 429, "We do not proclaim a deified Man, but we confess an incarnate God."[232]

Jesus could be our Savior only by being the Son of God, an incarnate God, both divine and human, born of the Virgin Mary. He received this "power" not from his legal father but from His Father in Heaven. No one other than the God-Man could ever take away the sins of the world. It was Jesus' divine nature that gave His Crucifixion a universal significance. In other words, the power of Jesus' Crucifixion was possible only through the mystery of His Incarnation — the coming of God in the flesh and joining us in our valley of tears.

That's the reason Christians revere the Blood of Jesus — not because of its blood type or its DNA but because of its redeeming power, which was made possible by His birth of the Virgin Mary. St. Peter says, "You were ransomed from the futile ways inherited from your forefathers ... with the precious blood of Christ, like that of a lamb without blemish or spot."[233] Or as St. Paul says, "For in him all the fullness of God was pleased to dwell, and through him to reconcile to himself all things, whether on earth or in heaven, making peace by the blood of his cross."[234] The blood Jesus shed on the Cross was the price paid for the sins of all mankind. No wonder the Shroud of Turin is seen as a testimony to that price of redemption.

So, how could the Virgin Birth be possible? We shouldn't look to genetics, nor its geneticists, for our answer. The Virgin Birth is not a genetic issue, so we found out. Geneticists' answers would be at best pseudoscientific, but certainly not religious, theological,

---

[232] Proclus of Constantinople, *Sermon on the Annunciation.*
[233] 1 Pet. 1:18–19.
[234] Col. 1:19–20.

or biblical. Our Catholic Faith would simply disappear into the scientific mists. What, then, was it that makes the Virgin Birth possible, if it's not science or genetics? There is only one answer: God's omnipotence. Why would God, who created the entire universe out of nothing, not be able to enable the Virgin Birth? Isn't that what we call a miracle?

Miracles and Mysteries

You might wonder how we can even bring up miracles after explaining that science and reason can never claim what is against religion and faith, while religion and faith can never claim anything that is against science or reason. Aren't miracles a direct denial of what science tells us?

Many people think so. The atheist and biologist Richard Dawkins, for instance, encapsulated the general opinion when he said, "Miracles, by definition, violate the principles of science."[235] This shows again the thorough permeation of scientism in the culture. We will discuss in the next chapter why scientism cannot be true. For now, I would say only that science does not have the tools, the expertise, or the authority to declare that miracles are impossible.

The argument that miracles are impossible was made almost three centuries ago by David Hume. He defined a miracle as "a transgression of a law of nature."[236] How strong or weak is his argument? The truth of the matter is that scientific research and

---

[235] Richard Dawkins, *The God Delusion* (Boston: Mariner Books, 2008), 83.
[236] David Hume, *An Enquiry Concerning Human Understanding* X, i, 90.

our knowledge about the natural world and how it operates could not even in principle show that miracles are impossible. The stock argument that skeptics such as Hume use is that miracles are violations of the laws of nature. These skeptics, however, hold at least one hidden assumption, which says that there is only one world: a natural world, and therefore, no supernatural world. This excludes miracles beforehand. You can only conclude that miracles are impossible if you presume beforehand that the supernatural world cannot or does not exist and thereby cannot intervene in the natural world. But isn't that the whole question in the first place? Apparently, the idea that miracles are impossible is based on a presupposition that what it is trying to prove is already true.

Once we question such a presumption—and we should—we must revise the way we understand miracles and the laws of nature. To begin with, we need a better definition of miracle. C. S. Lewis provides one: "I use the word Miracle to mean an interference with Nature by supernatural power."[237] Second, we need to better understand what the laws of nature entail: processes that naturally and consistently occur when all extraneous factors are held constant. For instance, the law of gravity tells us that a ball will fall to the ground every time we drop it, but that doesn't mean someone may stop this from happening by catching the ball before it hits the ground. Catching the ball is an interfering, extraneous factor.

The laws of nature manifest themselves only when certain conditions are met; put more technically, they have a clause of *ceteris paribus* (all things being equal). A law of nature states what is the case if, and only if, all other factors are held constant. But

---

[237] C. S. Lewis, *Miracles* (London: Harper Collins, 1947), 5.

what about supernatural factors such as God's interference? What of intervening factors of the *supernatural* kind? That's basically the point Lewis is making: miracles are interventions of the supernatural world in the natural world. He argues that miracles go beyond natural law, yet they are consistent with nature.[238] If God does not have power over matter (matter that He created), then He simply is not God.

Seen this way, a miracle does not prove a law of nature to be false or violated, but simply indicates that there is a supernatural cause, coming from faith, in addition to and beyond the natural causes. Rather than breaking laws of nature, God allows His miracles to transcend them. It is not a matter of believing in *either* miracles *or* science; it is a matter of accepting in faith that God as Creator has the authority to work within that nature in a way that cannot be reasoned through natural sciences. Rejecting the false dichotomy between faith and reason leaves science as well as religion standing. Miracles belong to the domain of religion, whereas laws of nature belong to the domain of science. Again, good fences make good neighbors.

This takes us to a closely related issue. It is quite common among Christians to connect miracles with mysteries. Here are a few examples of mysteries in the Catholic Faith: the Holy Trinity, the Incarnation, the Virgin Birth, the Eucharist, the Resurrection, and the Ascension. Mysteries can be grasped to a limited degree, but they cannot be understood entirely. One can read Aquinas and gain a much better grasp of the nature of the Trinity, but even Aquinas didn't understand everything about the mystery. Although ultimately, mysteries of faith may be beyond our reason, they cannot go against reason. They can

[238] Ibid., 87.

be explained and defended but not proven, of course. But we must not let the inability to grasp mysteries completely stop us from contemplating them. Pondering the Incarnation and the Virgin Birth acts as a spiritual exercise that strengthens faith and inspires wonder in the glory of God. It also serves as a reminder of humility: our human intellects cannot compare with the infinite wisdom of God. We are not meant to understand all the mysteries of the world, but we may, and should, continue to contemplate them in faith.

The mystery of the Incarnation, for instance, tells us that Jesus was the God-Man who made our redemption possible through His suffering, Crucifixion, and death, but it doesn't give us the details of how this God-Man could be conceived of the Virgin Mary. That's the mystery and the miracle of the Incarnation; without it, the Shroud of Turin would just be a piece of cloth.

Once again, Lewis could not have expressed it better:

> The Christian story is precisely the story of one grand miracle, the Christian assertion being that what is beyond all space and time, what is uncreated, eternal, came into nature, into human nature, descended into His own universe, and rose again, bringing nature up with Him. It is precisely one great miracle. If you take that away there is nothing specifically Christian left.[239]

This should put scientific techniques such as DNA analysis in the right perspective: science may tell us many a thing but not everything. Take science for what it's worth, and put it in its right place. So we should not leave the Shroud of Turin in the

---

[239] C. S. Lewis, "The Grand Miracle," in *God in the Dock, Essays on Theology and Ethics* (Grand Rapids: Eerdmans, 1972), 80.

laboratory but expose it to all the faithful through photographs, videos, and books. In this act of sharing, the Shroud comes alive and tells us more than science can on its own.

We must come to the conclusion that science does not have the last word, not even in DNA analysis, when it comes to the Shroud of Turin. What we do discover through science should not contradict what our Faith reveals but can confirm it. Our Faith might even add new insights that are beyond the scope of the DNA analysis.

Conclusion

Is the Shroud a hoax? If it is not, then is it from the time of Jesus? If it is from the time of Jesus, then is it from Jesus Himself? Science has offered to help us find answers to such questions. Well, it has actually *demanded* to find answers to such questions. Has science played its role reliably and honestly? In this book, we sought to define that role, while exploring the various means of authenticating the Shroud of Turin.

What Is the Bottom Line?

Biblical analysis has shown us that Jesus, in the words of the Apostles' Creed, "suffered under Pontius Pilate, was crucified, died, and was buried." His Crucifixion was carried out the way Roman crucifixions typically were carried out. They were very cruel executions that tried to delay death so the victim could be tortured, scourged, and mocked as much as possible. For Christians, the Passion and death are an essential part of Jesus' life and a central event in salvation history. They faithfully portray Jesus in historical terms, making Him essential to human history. This could be one of the best antidotes against the heresy of Docetism. Crucifixion, shameful as the method of execution is, has become an essential part of the Christian message. It represents the saving power of God through the total sacrifice of His Son, Jesus. Seen in this light, the Shroud of Turin shows us in gruesome detail the price at which our redemption was bought.

Historical analysis has revealed that there is reasonable evidence for the route of the Shroud to have led from Jerusalem to Turin. Some historians may attack the evidence, but the problem arises when historians treat historical facts as only that which is etched in stone. However, facts are not material entities that can be hauled into the laboratory. Tracing the path of the Shroud of Turin may not be possible in minute detail, but the general line is there. We discussed why we cannot use missing records to claim the truth of a universal negative. We also discussed that there are some gaps in the sequence of events, but these are rather an issue of "absence of evidence" than "evidence of absence." The long sequence of events connecting the Shroud of Turin to the Shroud of Jerusalem thus remains standing.

Computer analysis makes it possible to extract more detailed information from the Shroud of Turin, since much of the information it contains is hidden from the naked eye. Many techniques have become available, starting with simple photography, followed by high-definition, computer-aided photography, and eventually aerospace technologies for developing 3D images. The best way to view the Shroud is to see it as a negative image of the body wrapped within. These new scientific techniques give us information that we would not have known otherwise. In general, though, they confirm what biblical and historical analysis had told us already.

Anatomical analysis reveals that the man in the Shroud is a grown male, standing five feet eleven inches tall, with shoulder length hair and a beard. The blood marks indicate that the man suffered great physical injury. Their placement on the head, hand, and feet aligns with the practice of crucifixion, implicating that this was one such victim. The wound at the side aligns with the Gospels' account detailing the piercing of the side of Christ, giving evidence that the image might depict our Lord Himself. The scientific controversies about these findings only show us that nothing in science is final or definitive. Science is always a work in progress. Even anatomical facts are not etched in stone but remain open for discussion, often acting as hypotheses in need of further confirmation.

Textile analysis teaches us that the linens were handmade by a professional—something that only a wealthier person, such as Joseph of Arimathea, would have been able to afford. The flax plant from which the fibers came are traced not to Europe but rather to the Eastern Mediterranean or the Middle East. The stitching observed along the side strip, being nearly identical to an artifact found at Masada in Israel, further confirms the location of origin of the material as well as establishing an approximate time frame for the cloth between 40 BC and AD 73. Tests on the Shroud's vanillin content reveal that it could be as old as the linen wrappings of the Dead Sea Scrolls, dated between 300 BC and AD 300. All this data makes it highly likely that it is not only a shroud of Judea but also the Shroud of Jesus.

Pollen analysis is based on studying pollen grains under the microscope—preferably under an electron scanning microscope. The shape, size, and markings of the pollen's surface can help us determine the genus, or sometimes the species, of the grains found on the Shroud. If we know the habitat of the plants belonging to that genus or species—on the assumption that their habitat hasn't changed since—then we can deduce that the Shroud must have been near Jerusalem at some point. We came to the conclusion, however, that pollen analysis has too many caveats, and therefore cannot really prove that the cloth was in Judea. But neither can it disprove that the Shroud of Turin was once there either.

Carbon analysis gave us one of the greatest shocks regarding the Shroud investigation. In 1988, a group of scientists declared—presumably in the name of science and sealed with their scientific authority—that the Shroud of Turin could not be dated earlier than 1260, making it a medieval forgery. What they didn't mention is that their findings and conclusions came with many questionable assumptions, which are common pitfalls of scientific research. We found many reasons pointing to the unreliability of the dating; the main one being that these scientists had tested a piece of the cloth that had been added to the Shroud later. It cannot prove that the Shroud is relatively recent, nor can it disprove that the Shroud is from the time of Jesus.

Blood analysis, through chemical and biological testing, reveals that there are indeed bloodstains on the Shroud. There is an abundance of evidence that these spots are not the work of an artist or a forger. The idea that the Shroud is a painted linen is just a hypothesis—one that has yet to be backed by supporting evidence. Further research has suggested that the person buried in the cloth had an AB blood type with an MNS blood type. Whether this information is important to know for people who venerate the Shroud of Turin as the burial cloth of Jesus is another question. But it does further validate the claim that we are dealing with real human blood on the Shroud of Turin, not just paint strokes.

DNA analysis has shown that the person buried in the Shroud was a man who had a Y chromosome. Where his Y chromosome came from is impossible to tell. According to Scripture, the Virgin Birth prohibits Jesus' Y chromosome from coming from His legal father, Joseph. This leaves the origin of the Y chromosome a mystery, if the man in the Shroud is indeed Jesus of Nazareth, the Son of God. This phenomenon raises the question of whether such a miracle is possible, and if so, how it could be. Science has no answer, but we made clear that miracles such as these are not violations of scientific law, nor incompatible with the nature of the universe.

When taken together, these analyses make it hard to deny that the Shroud of Turin is, in fact, the Shroud of Jesus. Continued studies offer more evidence for its validity, although they also open new fields of questioning along the way. Indeed, the Shroud keeps surprising us. Its best surprise is that it might very well be the Shroud of Jesus that survived persecutions, fires, mishandling, and scientific scrutiny.

Does Science Have the Last Word?

Science does not have the last word—period! There is so much that science can do for us, but there is also so much that science is incapable of doing for us. That's the main reason it simply cannot have the last word.

There is no need to show what science *can* do for us. Most people are very aware of the impressive track record it has acquired. We also saw in this book that science can help us discover things about the Shroud we would not have known otherwise—specifically, by using DNA analysis, blood analysis, carbon analysis, pollen analysis, textile analysis, anatomical analysis, and computer analysis. Kudos to science!

On the other hand, many people are unaware of that which science *cannot* do for us, despite its numerous remarkable achievements. Here are some of the things that science cannot do for us:

A Catholic Scientist Champions the Shroud of Turin

1. Science *cannot* prove much with final certainty, as I have mentioned repeatedly in this book. Yes, mathematics can prove things with final certainty, but science cannot. In geometry, for example, one can prove that the sum of the three angles of a triangle is 180 degrees. But such a proof is possible only if one accepts the axioms on which the proof lies. Based on a set of axioms in the premises, one can derive a conclusion with final certainty. Hence, the certainty of the conclusion is based on the presumed certainty of the axioms. But science does not work with axioms that are certain.

Science instead works with confirmation at best but never with final certainty. The discussion between scientists begins by questioning the claims of those on the other side of the debate. This method explains why scientists continually question the findings made by other scientists. The questioning procedure itself indicates that we have no reason to expect a final answer from science about the authenticity of the Shroud either. Science cannot prove that the Shroud is *not* from Jesus, nor can it prove with certainty that it *is*. Science does not have the power to attain complete confirmation, nor can it attain definitive falsification. There is always room for revisiting and revising.

Even if science cannot prove that the Shroud of Turin is the shroud in which Jesus was buried, so what? If Christians believe that the Shroud of Turin is the Shroud of Jesus, they may have very good reasons to do so. This book offers a long series of such reasons. The reasons also show that science doesn't necessarily have the last word; it cannot claim to have the final truth about the Shroud of Turin.

2. Science *cannot* prove that science itself is the only way of finding truth. There is no experiment and no empirical evidence that could do the trick. We cannot test this claim in

the laboratory or with a double-blind experiment. Ironically, the claim "no statements are true unless they can be proven scientifically" cannot itself be proven scientifically. This claim that "all questions have scientific answers" is an example of a *universal positive* ("all Xs are Ys")—an unending proposition that is logically impossible to prove. Science on its own cannot answer questions that are beyond the reach of its empirical and experimental techniques. Even if there are many scientific answers to many of our questions, "many" does not equate to "all."

To keep claiming that science can answer all our questions is not a scientific discovery, but at best a philosophical or metaphysical viewpoint, called scientism—and a poor one at that. It declares everything outside science as a despicable form of metaphysics, in defiance of the fact that all those who reject metaphysics are, in fact, committing their own version of metaphysics. This means that science doesn't necessarily have the last word; for instance, it cannot claim to have scientific answers to all our questions about the Shroud of Turin.

3. Science *cannot* claim that the field of science encapsulates all there is in this universe. The reason this claim cannot be true is that one cannot talk *about* science without stepping *outside* science. Stating that science covers all there is, and that there can be nothing outside it, is a claim necessarily made from outside the domain of science, thus grossly overstepping its own boundaries. By doing so, it loses the very scientific credentials it so wants to defend. The claim that there is nothing outside science and that there is no point of view other than the scientific one can be made only by doing exactly that which it prohibits—namely, stepping outside science.

Making a statement from outside the domain of science cannot be tested with tools and methods from inside the domain of science. Science cannot pull itself up by its own bootstraps—any more than an electric generator is able to run on its own power. This means that science doesn't necessarily have the last word; for instance, it cannot claim that only science is capable of talking sensibly about the Shroud of Turin.

4. Science *cannot* discard worldviews and explanations on the basis that they are not founded in science or validated scientifically. To put this in a catchphrase, science cannot reject what it has chosen to neglect. Lung physiologists, for instance, may neglect genetics as not being part of their expertise, but that does not entitle them to reject genetics as a legitimate scientific field.

Something similar can be said about religious statements: scientists usually neglect them in their research, but they cannot reject them for that reason. They may be able to neglect or ignore religious facts and explanations, but they cannot logically and validly conclude that they must be rejected as unreasonable or unfounded, let alone as nonexistent, as a result. Something we neglect we cannot just reject, unless we have additional reasons for doing so. If those additional reasons are missing, there is still room left for explanations other than scientific ones.

The late philosopher of science at UC Berkeley Paul Feyerabend agreed when he said, "Science should be taught as one view among many and not as the one and only road to truth and reality."[240] Even the "positivistic" philosopher Gilbert Ryle expressed a similar view: "The nuclear physicist, the theologian, the historian, the lyric poet and the man in the street produce very different, yet compatible and even complementary pictures

---

[240] Paul Feyerabend, *Against Method: Outline of an Anarchistic Theory of Knowledge* (New York: Verso Books, 1975), viii.

of one and the same 'world.'"[241] Science provides only one of these views. This means that science doesn't necessarily have the last word; for instance, it cannot claim to have the only valid explanations about the Shroud of Turin.

5. Science *cannot* declare its own methodology superior, and then disqualify all others by claiming (in an unscientific way) that *its* methodology is the *only* legitimate and reliable one that the world has to offer. A blood test, for instance, is an excellent method to assess a person's health. There are many other reliable methods, however, such as X-rays and MRIs, depending on what exactly we are trying to assess. But a blood test on its own cannot be used to prove that a blood test is the best, let alone the only, method there is. Not surprisingly, this misconception of science often results from hyperspecialized training coupled with a lack of exposure to other disciplines.

An image used by the late psychologist Abraham Maslow might be helpful here: if you only have a hammer, every problem begins to look like a nail.[242] The truth of the matter is that our world is not made only of nails. So, instead of idolizing our "scientific hammer," we should acknowledge that not everything is a "nail." Even if we were to agree that the scientific method generally gives us better, more testable results, this would not mean that the scientific method alone gives us genuine knowledge of reality. This means, once again, that science doesn't necessarily have the last word; for instance, it cannot claim to have the only valid truth about the Shroud of Turin.

---

[241] Gilbert Ryle, *Dilemmas* (Cambridge, MA: Cambridge University Press, 1954), 80.

[242] A. H. Maslow, *The Psychology of Science* (New York: HarperCollins, 1966), 15.

6. Science *cannot* claim that what science reveals is literally all there is. Consider the analogy used by the philosopher Edward Feser: a metal detector is a perfect tool to locate metals, but that does not mean there is nothing more to this world than metals.[243] A metal detector is not a good tool to find plastic cups on the beach, for instance. This tool gives us only a very limited form of knowledge. Those who object to this analogy on the grounds that metal detectors detect only part of reality, while science detects the whole of it, are simply begging the question again—whether science really does describe the whole of reality.

An instrument can detect only what it is designed to detect—and this is exactly where the monopolistic view of science goes wrong. Instead of letting reality determine which techniques are appropriate in which cases, the claim that only science can show us what is real essentially lets one favorite technique dictate all "reality." This belief denies the fact that science has purchased success at the cost of limiting its ambition. This means that science doesn't necessarily have the last word; for instance, it cannot claim to have the best, nor only, analysis about the Shroud of Turin.

7. Science *cannot* claim that there are only material entities in the world. The reason for this is very simple: science limits itself, by definition, to what is material—to what can be measured, weighed, counted, and quantified. Due to the bounds of its own definition, science then cannot go beyond itself by claiming that everything else in this world must be material too. Put differently, after science limits itself exclusively to what can be measured, counted, and quantified, it declares everything that

---

[243] Edward Feser, *Scholastic Metaphysics: A Contemporary Introduction* (Havertown, PA: Editions Scholasticae, 2014), section 0.2.4.

cannot be measured, counted, or quantified as nonexistent. It is circular reasoning. The late philosopher Ralph Barton Perry exposed its circularity as follows: "A certain type of method is accredited by its applicability to a certain type of fact; and this type of fact, in turn, is accredited by its lending itself to a certain type of method."[244] That's how we keep circling around.

If everything in this world were indeed material, then we would not be able to make the claim that everything is material, as claims are nonmaterial entities. Consequently, claims we make—such as the one that everything is material—cannot even exist in a world of material things. Therefore, the claim against immateriality itself acts as a kind of boomerang that comes back to hit whoever launched it. Albert Einstein is often quoted as having said, "Not everything that can be counted counts; not everything that counts can be counted."[245] There is so much that is not material in this world. This means that science doesn't necessarily have the last word; for instance, it cannot claim that the Shroud of Turin is only a tangible material, a linen cloth.

8. Science *cannot* prove that all our questions are scientific questions and will have scientific answers. There is just no way science on its own can demonstrate that it has an answer to all our questions. This would be possible only if we knew all the possible questions people might have, but also all the answers that science would come up with. That is a task without end; it's

---

[244] Ralph Barton Perry, *Present Philosophical Tendencies* (New York: Longmans, Green, 2010), 81.

[245] It is often said this quote was written on a sign or blackboard in Einstein's office at Princeton University, but the claim is unsubstantiated. The quote is probably more recent and came perhaps from William Bruce Cameron.

a universal positive that cannot be proven. Yet, it is a perpetual dream of some scientists. It is in this frame of mind that the late cosmologist Stephen Hawking once exclaimed, "Our goal is a complete understanding of the events around us and of our own existence."[246]

Instead, one could agree with the late Nobel laureate and biologist Konrad Lorenz, who said that a scientist "knows more and more about less and less and finally knows everything about nothing."[247] Science on its own is not able to prove that it has answers to anything we might ask. The Austrian physicist and Nobel laureate Erwin Schrödinger once said about science, "It knows nothing of beautiful and ugly, good or bad, God and eternity."[248] This means that science doesn't necessarily have the last word; for instance, it cannot claim to have answers to all our questions about the Shroud of Turin.

9. Science *cannot* deal with anything in scientific terms beyond its own domain. The first legendary pioneers of science in England were very much aware of the fact that there is more to life than science. When the Royal Society of London was founded in 1660, its members explicitly demarcated their area of investigation and realized very clearly that they were going to leave many other domains untouched. In its charter, King Charles II assigned to the fellows of the society the privilege of enjoying intelligence and knowledge, but with the following

---

[246] Stephen Hawking, *A Brief History of Time* (New York: Bantam Books, 1998), 186.

[247] Quoted in Larry Collins and Thomas Schneid, *Physical Hazards of the Workplace* (Boca Raton, FL: CRC Press, 2001), 107.

[248] Erwin Schrödinger, *Nature and the Greeks in Nature and the Greeks and Science and Humanism* (Cambridge, MA: Cambridge University Press, 1964), 96.

important stipulation: "provided in matters of things philosophical, mathematical, and mechanical."[249] ("Philosophical" meant "scientific" back then.) That's how the domains of knowledge were separated; it was this "partition" that led to a division of labor between the sciences and other fields of human interest.

By accepting this separation, science bought its own territory, but certainly at the expense of all-inclusiveness; the rest of the "estate" was reserved for others to manage. On the one hand, it gave to scientists all that could be solved "methodically" by dissecting, counting, and measuring. On the other hand, these scientists agreed to keep their hands off all other domains—education, legislation, justice, ethics, and certainly religion—because those require a different "expertise." Therefore, scientists, in their role as scientists, must keep their hands off anything beyond their reach. This means that science doesn't necessarily have the last word; for instance, it cannot claim to have the final say about the Shroud of Turin. Science can show us things about the Shroud we would not know otherwise, but there are also things about the Shroud beyond science's domain.

10. Science *cannot* explain anything supernatural by transforming it into something natural. It cannot explain issues such as the Incarnation, the Virgin Birth, the Resurrection,

---

[249] The Royal Society originated on November 28, 1660, when twelve men met to set up "a Colledge for the promoting of Physico-Mathematicall Experimentall Learning." Robert Hooke's draft of its statutes reads: "The Business and Design of the Royal Society is: To improve the knowledge of natural things, and all useful Arts, Manufactures, Mechanik practices, Engyries and Inventions by Experiments—(not meddling with Divinity, Metaphysics, Moralls, Politicks, Grammar, Rhetorik, or Logic)."

the Redemption, and so on. Almost everyone agrees at first, until we find out what people conclude from this, then the division sets in.

On the one hand, there are the ones who say the supernatural doesn't exist and cannot exist—and that's why science cannot explain them. They see the world as a gigantic machine in which everything that happens must have a natural, mechanistic explanation, leaving no room for the supernatural. When people say, "I know there must be some natural explanation for X," they don't actually *know*; they make an assumption based on their worldview. The problem is, though, that we believe far too much on no better ground than that it is what "everybody knows." But this belief is as much faith as any belief taught by a church.

On the other hand, there are those who accept and believe in supernatural explanations in addition to natural ones. Even if science cannot explain the Resurrection, this doesn't mean that there is no Resurrection. As we found out, science doesn't have the power to explain the unexplainable by denying its existence. There are definitely immaterial truths that cannot be ignored or denied by science. Just think of logic and mathematics—two immaterial fields without which science would not be possible.

Logic and mathematics are not material and physical, and therefore not testable by the empirical sciences. Yet, in logic and mathematics, immaterial things are true and demonstrable, even though they are beyond scientific observation. Why couldn't the same be true of supernatural phenomena? I see no reason why not. Just as there is good and bad logic, there is also good and bad religion, reasonable and unreasonable religion. This means that science doesn't necessarily have the last word; for instance, it cannot claim that the Shroud of Turin cannot be the burial cloth that once held the body of the resurrected Jesus.

Having seen all the above, we must conclude that science may have done a lot for the study of the Shroud of Turin, but this doesn't take away from the fact that there is a lot that science *cannot* do. Most scientists we mentioned in this book have a certain "professional" attitude of acting like detached, scientific observers who have no personal connection with the Shroud. They merely observe and study the cloth. The detached approach may be very appropriate during their scientific research, but there also may be a time that they should step out of their comfort zone—for the simple reason that science doesn't have the only, let alone the last, word.

Is the Shroud an Icon or a Relic?

Most believers have their own opinion about what the Shroud of Turin means to them. For some, it's a relic; for others, an icon. Are Catholics supposed to go one way or the other? It may come as a surprise to many, but the Catholic Church has never formally endorsed or rejected the Shroud of Turin as a relic.

After Pope Paul VI had called the Shroud "the greatest relic in Christendom,"[250] the next three popes made some rather neutral comments about it. John Paul II spoke in terms of an "icon" when he said in his 1998 address in Turin, "The imprint left by the tortured body of the Crucified One, which attests to the tremendous human capacity for causing pain and death to one's fellow man, stands as an icon of the suffering of the innocent

[250] *U.S. Catholic* (May 1978): 48.

in every age."[251] During the same address, he also spoke of the Shroud as "a mirror of the Gospel."

Pope Benedict XVI also used the term "icon" in his message for a display of the Shroud on May 2, 2010. He spoke of "this extraordinary Icon," "the Icon of Holy Saturday," and "an Icon written in blood; the blood of a man who was scourged, crowned with thorns, crucified and whose right side was pierced."[252] But he also added, "Indeed it is a winding-sheet that was wrapped round the body of a man who was crucified, corresponding in every way to what the Gospels tell us of Jesus." That comes at least closer to a relic than an icon.

On March 20, 2013, Pope Francis used the term "icon" in a video message in which he called the Shroud the "icon of a man scourged and crucified." He added, "This image, impressed upon the cloth, speaks to our heart and moves us to climb the hill of Calvary, to look upon the wood of the Cross, and to immerse ourselves in the eloquent silence of love."[253] During his June 21, 2015, visit to Turin, he prayed in front of the Shroud and called it "an icon of love."[254] These are rather vague spiritualized statements.

Why is the Catholic Church so agnostic regarding the authenticity of the Shroud? What makes her so reluctant to utter any more positive, official statements? There are some likely explanations. When John Paul II visited the Shroud in 1998, he said:

---

[251] Pastoral visit of Pope John Paul II to Vercelli and Turin, Italy, May 23–24, 1998.

[252] Pastoral visit of Pope Benedict XVI to Turin, May 2, 2010.

[253] Pope Francis, video message, March 30, 2013.

[254] Associated Press, "Pope Francis Praises Turin Shroud as an 'Icon of Love,'" *Guardian* (U.S. edition), https://www.theguardian.com/world/2015/jun/21/pope-francis-turin-shroud-icon-of-love.

The mysterious fascination of the Shroud forces questions to be raised about the sacred Linen and the historical life of Jesus. Since it is not a matter of faith, the Church has no specific competence to pronounce on these questions. She entrusts to scientists the task of continuing to investigate, so that satisfactory answers may be found to the questions connected with this Sheet, which, according to tradition, wrapped the body of our Redeemer after he had been taken down from the cross.[255]

The question of whether the Shroud of Turin is a relic or an icon is strongly connected with the common thread running through this entire book: What is the role of science in all of this?

On the one hand, the Catholic Church favors the unity of faith and reason, of religion and science. As we discussed at the beginning, this means that faith cannot go against reason, or reversed, and that religion cannot go against science. It also means that science and religion can live in harmony. It is the harmony between the two that leads us to the truth. Even though many people may feel a strong conflict between the idea that the Shroud as an object of religious adoration is set against the Shroud as an object of scientific investigation, these two approaches do not necessarily conflict with one another.

On the other hand, it appears that there have been conflicts between science and religion. Perhaps the best-known case is the Galileo affair. This conflict is usually portrayed in terms favorable to Galileo, but many false myths have surrounded the case. This cloud of myths obscures the real facts about Galileo: he did not discover that the earth is round; he did not invent

---

[255] Pastoral visit of Pope John Paul II to Vercelli and Turin.

the telescope; he was not the first to advance heliocentrism; he did not prove heliocentrism; he was not silenced by anti-scientists; he was not tortured by the Inquisition; he was not incarcerated by the Inquisition; he did not mutter, "And yet the earth moves." Instead, what was condemned by the Church was not so much Galileo the scientist and his astronomy, but Galileo the ideologue who had his own agenda and had been proclaiming himself an expert in theological matters. He was promoting a theory that seemingly contradicted Scripture, setting out to "disprove" the inerrant Word of God and prove his own scientific claims certain and true, but without having enough evidence to support them.[256]

Nevertheless, the Galileo conflict made Pope John Paul II extremely cautious about potential conflicts between science and religion. During a conference celebrating the 350th anniversary of the publication of Galileo's *Dialogue concerning the Two Chief World Systems*, the pontiff remarked that the experience of the Galileo case had led the Church "to a more mature attitude and a more accurate grasp of the authority proper to her," enabling her better to distinguish between "essentials of the faith" and the "scientific systems of a given age."[257] The pontiff called Galileo's run-in with the Church a "tragic mutual incomprehension" in which both sides were at fault. Although both Galileo and the Church were at fault, they also both learned from this experience.

---

[256] Gerard Verschuuren, *The Myth of an Anti-Science Church—Galileo, Darwin, Teilhard, Hawking, Dawkins* (Kettering, OH: Angelico Press, 2019), 27–36.

[257] John Paul II, Address to an International Symposium on the occasion of the 350th anniversary of the publication of Galileo's Dialogue concerning the Two Chief World Systems, May 9, 1983.

Pope John Paul II himself had learned from this experience too. I quoted him earlier in this chapter, stating that the Church has no competence in matters of science—a sound position.[258] This "policy" explains why the Catholic Church has never declared scientific issues a matter of dogma. She will never declare the Big Bang or heliocentrism or evolution a dogma to be held by all the faithful because these are issues outside her territory; they are not matters of faith or morals.

Is not the authenticity of the Shroud of Turin a similar issue? Perhaps it is. But in this case, the situation is a bit different. When the Vatican calls the Shroud an "icon" rather than a "relic," it recognizes its symbolic importance without taking a stand on whether it is historically and scientifically authentic.

However, the case could be made instead that the reputation of the Shroud of Turin has been damaged by many scientific researchers. The team that radiocarbon-dated the Shroud of Turin, for instance, probably did the most damage to the Shroud by rejecting its authenticity "in the name of science." They never showed awareness of the pitfalls of radiocarbon dating; they may not even have been aware of the limitations of science in general. The results of the few scientists who performed the radiocarbon dating turned out to be very questionable, as we discussed earlier. Perhaps the Shroud is not a hoax, but their scientific verdict was.

Although many others have joined the growing crowd of skeptics, the authenticity of the Shroud of Turin is still standing, even among quite a few scientists. Philip Ball, former editor of *Nature*, hinted at the Shroud's enduring challenge: "It's fair to say that, despite the seemingly definitive tests in 1988, the status of the Shroud of Turin is murkier than ever. Not least, the nature

[258] Pastoral visit of Pope John Paul II to Vercelli and Turin.

of the image and how it was fixed on the cloth remain deeply puzzling."[259] The most amazing outcome is that the Shroud of Turin has outlasted so many challenges, including, as we have seen, Christian persecutions, fire damage, human mishandling, and scientific scrutiny.

Does this mean that the Shroud of Turin could still be a relic rather than an icon? The term "icon" may sound safe and neutral, but it is also quite meaningless. Icons are merely pictures made by human hands. They are representations of something else, expressed in black and white or in color, on linen, canvas, wood, or stone. If the figure seen on the Shroud of Turin were indeed a painting, then the Shroud would rightly be called an icon. But we discussed already the supreme lack of data supporting this hypothesis.

On the other hand, if the figure on the Shroud is the real imprint of the crucified body buried within the cloth, then it is a *relic* of that person. What makes a relic like this so precious is that it shows us what Jesus must have looked like — something icons of Jesus cannot do. It also shows clearly that the Crucifixion was the price Jesus paid for our redemption. Perhaps the Shroud of Turin gives us the same opportunity given to St. Thomas the Apostle after the Resurrection, when he said, "Unless I see in his hands the print of the nails, and place my finger in the mark of the nails, and place my hand in his side, I will not believe."[260] Perhaps the Shroud can make us believe.

Unfortunately, the pictures and icons of Jesus we know of reflect more about their makers than about Jesus. In Ireland, Jesus looks Irish; in Italy, He looks Italian; in China, He looks

[259] Philip Ball, "Shrouded in Mystery," *Nature, Materials* 7 (2008): 349.
[260] John 20:25.

Chinese; in Africa, He looks African. But hardly ever does He look Jewish. Does it matter? Not really. But if you want to come closer to "reality"—and we may want to, for Jesus was incarnated and became man through a Jewish virgin—then we may go for the now-famous image of the person in the Shroud of Turin. I personally think one of the best "icons" we can have of Jesus is the face we see on the Shroud of Turin. This face is arguably the best and most realistic icon of what Jesus looked like. But then it is no longer a mere icon but a real relic.

I often like to pray to Jesus with a picture or icon in front of me. Of course, I am not praying to a picture, but to Jesus with the help of His picture. It's like having a picture on your desk of your dear ones who have passed away. It's a welcome and helpful tool to remember them by. Even when we speak about Jesus and pray to Him, we "imagine" something about Him—not in pictures perhaps but at least in words. The Fourth General Council of Constantinople (869–870) makes this comparison: "What speech conveys in words, pictures announce and bring out in colors." Yes, as we all know, a picture can be worth a thousand words, but as a mere picture, it is still an icon, not a relic. The image on the Shroud is arguably the best "icon" we have of Jesus—but if the cloth *actually* touched His precious Body, and the image is *actually* a miraculous imprinting, then the Shroud is in fact a relic, a relic of Jesus of Nazareth, the Son of God.

As said before, the Shroud of Turin reveals to us Christ's payment for our salvation: He had to suffer and die for us. The Shroud shows us the cruel suffering of Jesus' Crucifixion and the depth of His passion and love—from the Agony in the Garden until His death on Calvary. In short, the Shroud of Turin is a silent witness of the Passion, death, and Resurrection of our Lord Jesus Christ. The poet Dante once famously asked, "My Lord,

Christ Jesus, God of very God, Now was your semblance made like unto this?"[261] Perhaps the Shroud of Turin gives us the answer.

I said it many times already—science can (and does) fail. For instance, when scientists, including Albert Einstein, said that the universe was eternal and had no beginning or end, the Church did not change her dogma that the universe was created "out of nothing" at some point in time and will have an end someday. Perhaps it's time for the Church to say something more definitive and positive about the Shroud so cherished and venerated by so many Christians. Perhaps this is where faith and reason, religion and science may nicely come together.

Let's close with this: when Barrie Schwortz, the famous photographer of the STURP team, asked his Jewish mother whether she thought the Shroud was authentic, she simply told him, "Barrie, of course it's authentic. They wouldn't have kept it for 2,000 years if it wasn't."[262]

[261] Dante Alighieri, *Paradiso*, Canto XXXI, The Literature Network, http://www.online-literature.com/dante/paradiso/31/.
[262] Adams, "Shroud of Turin."

Videos on the Shroud

If you want a list of Catholic videos on the Shroud of Turin, enter the following link into your browser in the top address line (not in the search box): *Bit.ly/ShroudVideos*.

For another rich selection of great videos, go to Formed (http://www.formed.org). Select "Sign up." You may want to start a free trial or pay for a membership subscription. (It may be worth checking beforehand to see whether your parish has a collective subscription.) In the search menu type "Shroud of Turin" to find all the videos Formed offers on the Shroud.

Index

About the Author

Gerard M. Verschuuren is a human biologist, specializing in human genetics. He also holds a doctorate in the philosophy of science. He studied and worked at universities in Europe and in the United States. Currently semiretired, he spends most of his time as a writer, speaker, and consultant on the interface of science and religion, faith and reason.

Some of his most recent books are: *How Science Points to God*; *In the Beginning: A Catholic Scientist Explains How God Made Earth Our Home*; *Forty Anti-Catholic Lies: A Mythbusting Apologist Sets the Record Straight*; *Darwin's Philosophical Legacy: The Good and the Not-So-Good*; *God and Evolution?: Science Meets Faith*; *The Destiny of the Universe: In Pursuit of the Great Unknown*; *It's All in the Genes!: Really?*; *Life's Journey: A Guide from Conception to Growing Up, Growing Old, and Natural Death*; *Aquinas and Modern Science: A New Synthesis of Faith and Reason*; *Faith and Reason: The Cradle of Truth*; *The Myth of an Anti-Science Church: Galileo, Darwin, Teilhard, Hawking, Dawkins*; and *At the Dawn of Humanity: The First Humans*.

For more information, visit https://en.wikipedia.org/wiki/Gerard_Verschuuren.

Verschuuren can be contacted at www.where-do-we-come-from.com.

Sophia Institute

Sophia Institute is a nonprofit institution that seeks to nurture the spiritual, moral, and cultural life of souls and to spread the Gospel of Christ in conformity with the authentic teachings of the Roman Catholic Church.

Sophia Institute Press fulfills this mission by offering translations, reprints, and new publications that afford readers a rich source of the enduring wisdom of mankind.

Sophia Institute also operates the popular online resource CatholicExchange.com. *Catholic Exchange* provides world news from a Catholic perspective as well as daily devotionals and articles that will help readers to grow in holiness and live a life consistent with the teachings of the Church.

In 2013, Sophia Institute launched Sophia Institute for Teachers to renew and rebuild Catholic culture through service to Catholic education. With the goal of nurturing the spiritual, moral, and cultural life of souls, and an abiding respect for the role and work of teachers, we strive to provide materials and programs that are at once enlightening to the mind and ennobling to the heart; faithful and complete, as well as useful and practical.

Sophia Institute gratefully recognizes the Solidarity Association for preserving and encouraging the growth of our apostolate over the course of many years. Without their generous and timely support, this book would not be in your hands.

www.SophiaInstitute.com
www.CatholicExchange.com
www.SophiaInstituteforTeachers.org

Sophia Institute Press® is a registered trademark of Sophia Institute. Sophia Institute is a tax-exempt institution as defined by the Internal Revenue Code, Section 501(c)(3). Tax ID 22-2548708.